What to do Till the Garbageman Arrives

A Miser's Craft Manual

Ruth Johnson

What to do Till the Garbageman Arrives

A Miser's Craft Manual

Gage Publishing

Gage Publishing
©Ruth Johnson

ISBN-0-7715-9950-I (Hardcover)
ISBN-0-7715-9951-X (Softcover)

Design by Fortunato Aglialoro
Illustrations by Jean Eugen

Printed and bound in Canada
2 3 4 5 GP 80 79

contents

introduction

This book is designed to show you how to put your garbage to work for you. It contains a collection of ideas and instructions for making useful objects and decorative crafts from the leavings of our society. It is a true miser's manual. The "throw-aways" or garbage used in these crafts are everyday items found in every householder's refuse. Only the simplest and most basic tools such as a hammer, saw, knife or scissors, are needed to make the various objects and the cost involved in their construction comes to no more than the money spent on the glue, tacks, tape, string, etc. necessary to put them together. There are no objects that start with a simple article and require the purchase of something complicated and expensive to complete it; nor is artistic talent required—the ideas are simple and easy-to-make—although those of you who have been blessed with creative talent will find that the ideas can be enlarged upon or reworked to become completely original. As an added bonus, most of the projects can be made by children with only an occasional assist from an adult. What better way to teach the new generation about the fun to be had and the money saved from reprogramming?

The re-use of discarded objects and garbage was something that our grandparents, and their parents before them, took for granted. It was part of their way of life. But our generation has been brainwashed into becoming a "throw-away" society. It is a sobering thought to realize that we belong to a culture where 20 percent of the world's population consumes 80 percent of the world's resources. It is obvious that reprogramming has become a *must*. And what better place to start than in the home? Next time you stand poised before the garbage can or wastebasket, *stop, think* and consider whether the object you are about to throw away could have another use. Could it be recycled into another existence and go full circle again?

I am an ordinary, run-of-the-mill housewife and mother, with a finger in community activities, a keen interest in ecology and a great hatred of waste. I started out as a garbage "watcher" which led me into recycling projects and finally into creating a collection of objects made from garbage. In this book I share some of my ideas with you and hope that you, and your children, will enjoy the fun of creating something useful and beautiful. I also hope that a new awareness of packaging and garbage pollution will creep into your daily life as you help to save the beauty around us by diminishing the mountains of garbage that mar the view and drain the economy.

By the way, no offence is meant to women by the use of "garbageman" in this book's title. "Garbage person," somehow lacks the proper rhythm, don't you think?

i tips for recyclers

Ask Yourself:

1. Do I really need this item?
2. Is it overpackaged? If so, peel off the excess and hand it to the store owner along with your opinion. Ask his support to influence his suppliers against overpackaging.
3. Do I avoid buying in plastic and buy in a more easily recycled glass or metal container?
4. Am I willing to buy beverages in returnable containers exclusively?

Home Checklist—Ask yourself:

1. Am I being wasteful of food? Have I used all that is possible?
2. Can I make something from the leftovers?
3. Can I share my excess?
4. Would a pet eat it?
5. Would it compost?
6. Can an article be mended or made over?
7. Is it of any use to someone else?
8. Is it good enough to be sold in a "next-to-new" shop managed by a service group?
9. Can it be made into something else and given a new life?
10. Will a container recycle?
    Glass—separate colored and clear; wash, remove metal.
    Cans—wash, remove label and flatten.
    Paper—separate clean wastepaper, corrugated and newspaper. Bundle securely with cord.

Check your local government for your closest recycling depot or neighborhood pick-up service, or open your own depot to service your area. If your area does not have facilities, bundle your paper products anyway. The technology is available to mechanically separate garbage and many localities are operating garbage reclamation plants. Paper can be recovered more efficiently from garbage dumped in such plants if it is securely bundled. The quality of the end product will be determined by the quality of the reclaimed paper. Each time paper is recycled the fibres break down and the quality of the paper steps down in grade. Good quality paper such as office paper, envelopes, etc., if unpolluted, can be made into a good quality bond. Paper can now be made from 100 percent recycled de-inked paper. Newsprint or low-grade paper can be recycled into products ranging from builders' tar paper, up to pressboard, cardboard, corrugated paper, and building blocks, as well as a very hard substance which can be utilized in the construction of wheels. It can also be mulched into a fertilizer or, with nutrients added, used as cattle fodder. The uses are many and varied and new ideas will yet appear. In areas where there is no feasible market for such paper products, it can be burned to generate steam which is sold as energy.

Did You Know

— that most neighborhoods have drop boxes for clothing, serviced by churches or service clubs?

— that appliances, furniture, etc. will be picked up and repaired by rehabilitation groups, and that proceeds from the sale of these articles make their income?

— that very worn garments bring revenue as rags for such organizations?

— that your small voice could start a chain reaction if you use it in your home and community to talk about pollution?

— that a letter written to the local, provincial and federal governments makes your opinion known? i.e., ban the non-returnable beverage container, restrict packaging, encourage garbage disposal by mechanical recycling and the burning of residue to create energy.

— that the opinion of you, the consumer, carries weight with the manufacturer if you let him know how you feel by phone or by letters to him and to the newspapers?

— that you could make it a neighborhood status symbol to have little or no garbage?

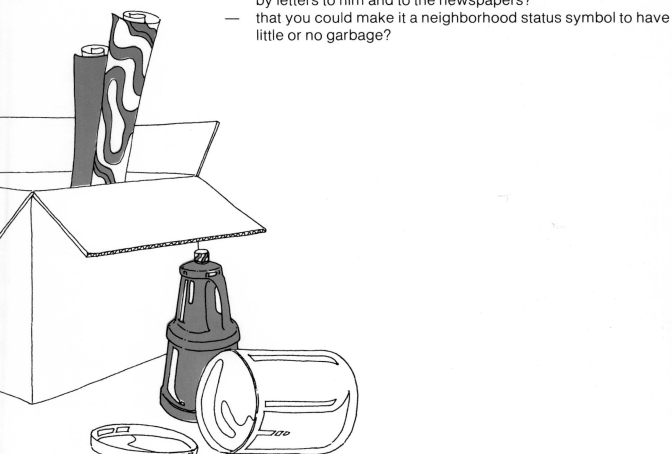

ii children's toys and games

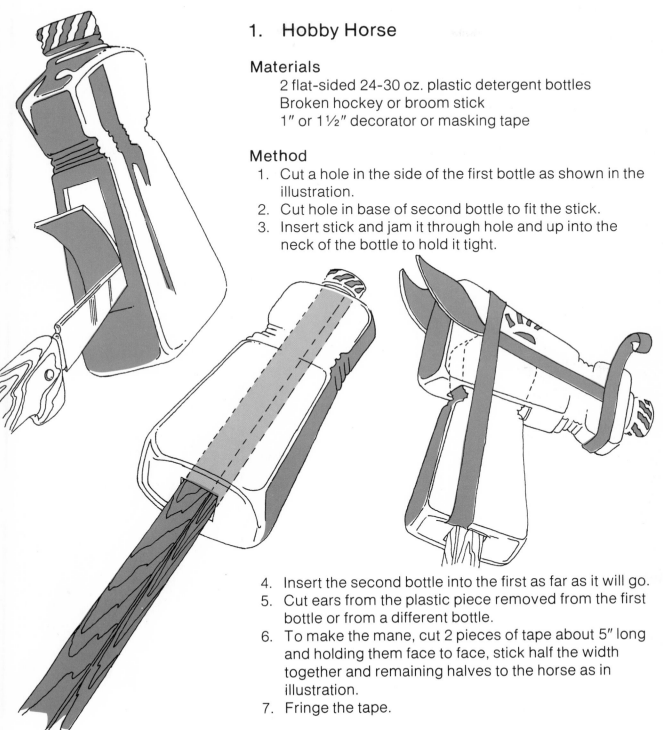

1. Hobby Horse

Materials
2 flat-sided 24-30 oz. plastic detergent bottles
Broken hockey or broom stick
1″ or 1½″ decorator or masking tape

Method
1. Cut a hole in the side of the first bottle as shown in the illustration.
2. Cut hole in base of second bottle to fit the stick.
3. Insert stick and jam it through hole and up into the neck of the bottle to hold it tight.
4. Insert the second bottle into the first as far as it will go.
5. Cut ears from the plastic piece removed from the first bottle or from a different bottle.
6. To make the mane, cut 2 pieces of tape about 5″ long and holding them face to face, stick half the width together and remaining halves to the horse as in illustration.
7. Fringe the tape.

5

8. Make mane for neck of horse using the same method.
9. Cut shapes for eyes, lashes and halter from tape and stick them in place.
10. If the young equestrian prefers riding at a gallop you may want to protect your floors from scuffs by binding the end of the stick with tape or by inserting the tip of the stick into an old sponge ball.

Hint

Many types of bottles would be suitable for your horse. The mane can also be made from yarn and the eyes from buttons. An old stuffed work sock makes a good head with the toe as muzzle and the leg as neck. Above all, recyclers, use your imagination and the materials available in your trash can.

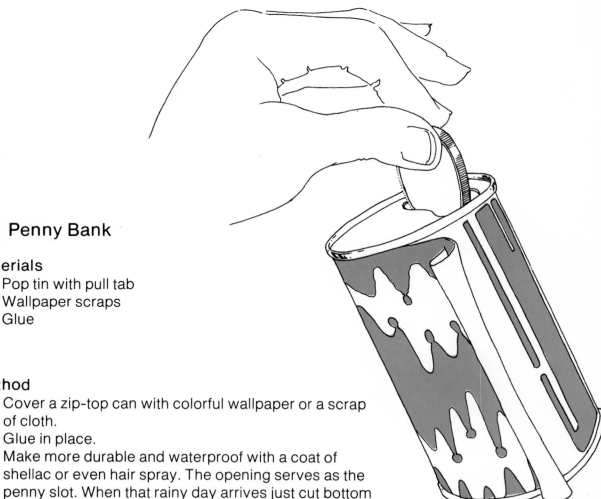

2. Penny Bank

Materials

Pop tin with pull tab
Wallpaper scraps
Glue

Method

1. Cover a zip-top can with colorful wallpaper or a scrap of cloth.
2. Glue in place.
3. Make more durable and waterproof with a coat of shellac or even hair spray. The opening serves as the penny slot. When that rainy day arrives just cut bottom from the can with a can opener to remove the loot.

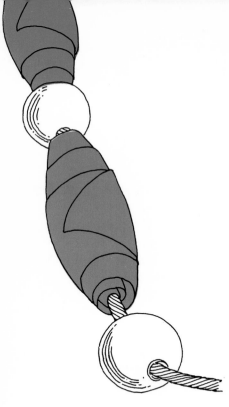

3. Beads

Materials
   Wallpaper or heavy colored paper from magazines
   Nylon stockings or cord

Method
1. Cut paper in long narrow triangle about 8" by 1".
2. Roll, wide base first, over a pencil for large bore beads, or over a knitting needle or toothpick for small bore beads.
3. Tip of the triangle should be glued to hold, then pencil removed.
4. The finished beads may be varnished, shellacked or given a coat of hair spray for protection and a glossy finish. They could also be painted.
5. String on cord or yarn.
6. If you wish spacers between the beads, cut old nylon stockings in spirals (this prevents running) and as you thread the beads on the nylon, tie loose knots between each bead to act as spacers. These can be made by craftsmen from 3 to 80 years of age.

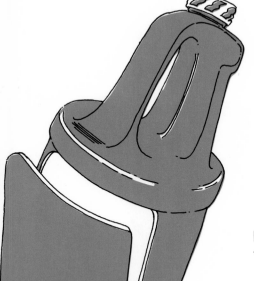

4. Sand Toys

A. Scoop
Materials

   Plastic bottle with side handle
   Knife

Method
1. Cut plastic bottle with sharp kitchen knife, holding it with handle to the top. The tip can be cut in a shape that is sharp or blunt to suit your purpose.

Hint
   Brightly colored plastic bottles work well for sand scoops because they are easily seen in the sand and the pliable plastic will not splinter or break.

B. Sand Pail
Materials

Plastic jug 64 oz. (or bigger)
Knife
1' of cord

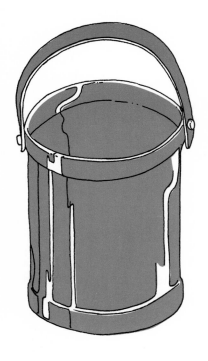

Method
1. Cut neck from jug with knife leaving only the base and sides.
2. Punch holes in each side opposite each other, about 1" from top, using an ice pick or knife.
3. For handle, insert cord in holes and knot it to hold. Or cut a strip about 1" wide for a handle from another bottle. Spread tacks punched through the handle and side of the pail will hold the handle in place.

C. Funnel
Materials

Round plastic bottle without handle about 1' high

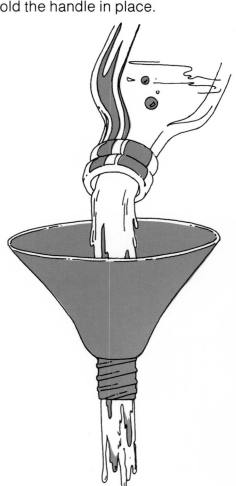

Method
1. Cut only the neck from the bottle and invert the neck. This will form your funnel.

Hint
A small child can pour water from container to container using the funnel while standing at the sink. This activity helps develop co-ordination and water play is very soothing. On rainy days or during winter you can make an indoor sand box by using coffee grounds that have been flushed clean after use, then dried. The tot can sit in the bathtub and pour, sift and make roads in a big flat pan. When he's finished playing just brush him off and swish spilled "sand" down the drain. Coffee grounds down the drain from time to time will absorb grease and oil.

5. Puppets

A. Sock Puppet
Materials

Odd sock
Sewing odds and ends such as colored yarn, felt or
    cloth strips
Buttons

Method

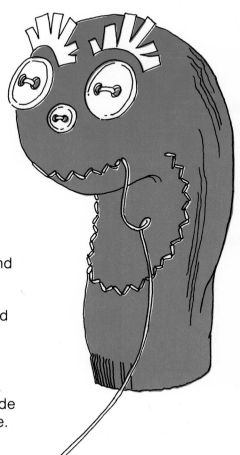

My family has a mysterious "sock stealer." As I am
sorting the laundry I always find one good sock with
no mate and nobody to blame. If the same thing
happens to you put the lone sock to good use as a
puppet. The following directions are for a simple,
easy-to-make puppet.

1. Put sock on your left hand if you are right-handed and
   the reverse if you aren't, so it will be easy for you to
   work with it.
2. Place your palm in the sole of the sock. As your hand
   closes decide where best to locate the mouth. It
   generally takes the whole sole for a mouth if the
   puppet is a cartoon-type creature.
3. Embroider a mouth, eyebrows and lashes with yarn.
   Use buttons for eyes. Tongue, teeth, etc. can be made
   by cutting strips of cloth or felt and sewing into place.
   Hair, if desired, can be made by looping strands of
   wool through the sock and tying it.

B. Mitt Puppet
Materials

Odd mitt (most families also have a mysterious mitt
    stealer)
Scraps similar to those used in Sock Puppet A

Method

1. Use the same method as for the sock puppet using
   your own variations. Cut off the thumb about halfway
   up and sew up the hole.
2. Using the thumb piece, make ears and sew on each
   side.

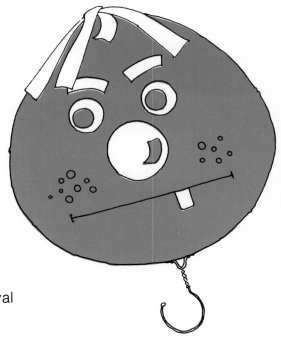

C. Nylon Puppet
Materials

> Nylon stocking
> Metal coat hanger
> Scissors
> Paint

Method
1. Bend the triangular part of the hanger into an oval shape.
2. Turn hook down to form handle.
3. Pull a nylon stocking over the oval and draw it up tight, tying just above the hook to hold it in place.
4. Paint a face on the oval section.
5. Make hair from another nylon cut in spiral strips, or yarn if you prefer.

D. Plastic-Bottle Puppet
1. **Simple**—easy for very young puppeteers to make.

Materials

> Plastic bottle such as the type used for dish detergent
> Old wool unravelled from sweater
> Glue
> Magic Markers
> Stick or wooden spoon

Method
1. Invert bottle and draw on a face with Magic Markers or by sticking on cutouts of colored tape.
2. Hair can be made from unravelled knitting wool or from nylons cut in a spiral and glued on the bottle head.
3. Insert the stick or wooden spoon into the neck of the bottle to use as a handle. The very young will find this fun to make and to use in play.

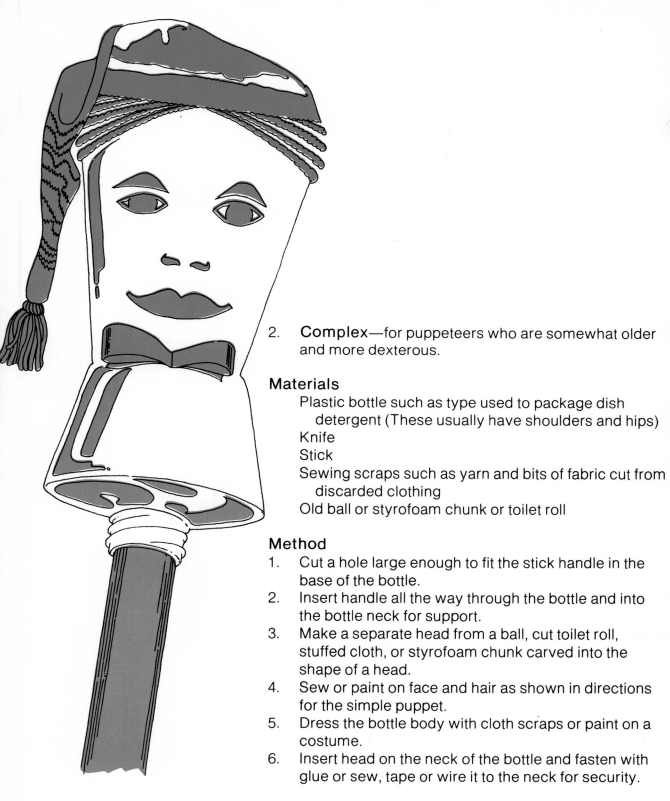

2. **Complex**—for puppeteers who are somewhat older and more dexterous.

Materials

    Plastic bottle such as type used to package dish
        detergent (These usually have shoulders and hips)
    Knife
    Stick
    Sewing scraps such as yarn and bits of fabric cut from
        discarded clothing
    Old ball or styrofoam chunk or toilet roll

Method

1. Cut a hole large enough to fit the stick handle in the base of the bottle.
2. Insert handle all the way through the bottle and into the bottle neck for support.
3. Make a separate head from a ball, cut toilet roll, stuffed cloth, or styrofoam chunk carved into the shape of a head.
4. Sew or paint on face and hair as shown in directions for the simple puppet.
5. Dress the bottle body with cloth scraps or paint on a costume.
6. Insert head on the neck of the bottle and fasten with glue or sew, tape or wire it to the neck for security.

6. Cannisters or Stacking Cans for Babies

Materials
Empty cans in graduated sizes with one end removed
Scraps of wallpaper or cloth
Glue
Shellac or varnish

Method
1. Check edges of cans for sharp catches. Running around the edges several times with a can opener will generally make the edge smooth. If not, file smooth with a round file.
2. Cover cans with wallpaper or cloth material and glue thoroughly. Cans can be stacked or nested together as an educational toy. Suggested sizes of cans from small to large: tomato paste, soup, cat food, tomatoes, beans.

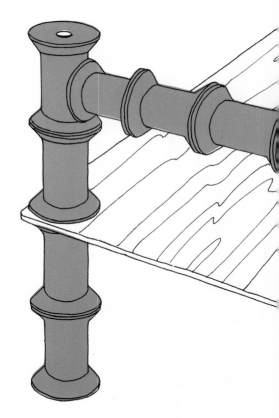

7. Storage Buckets for Toys

Materials
Cardboard bucket such as a potato chip or chicken bucket
Magazine pictures
Glue
Hair spray or shellac

Method
1. Decorate buckets with a collage of pictures in a theme that interests the child. To help him sort his own belongings, put a picture on the bucket that corresponds with the contents. i.e. picture of a car on the Dinky-Toy container, or of crayons on the crayon bucket.
2. To give a lasting finish to the bucket either varnish or spray with hair spray.

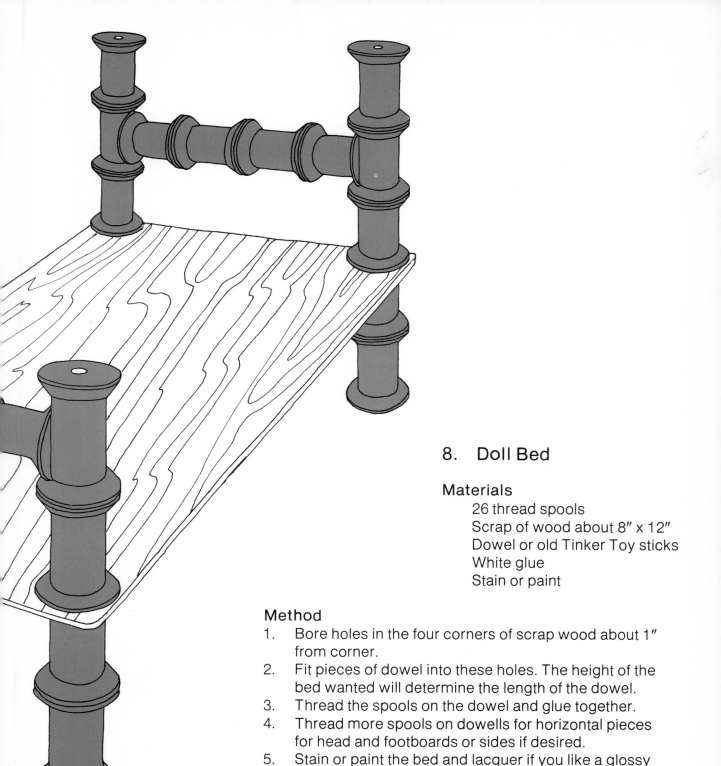

8. Doll Bed

Materials
    26 thread spools
    Scrap of wood about 8″ x 12″
    Dowel or old Tinker Toy sticks
    White glue
    Stain or paint

Method
1. Bore holes in the four corners of scrap wood about 1″ from corner.
2. Fit pieces of dowel into these holes. The height of the bed wanted will determine the length of the dowel.
3. Thread the spools on the dowel and glue together.
4. Thread more spools on dowells for horizontal pieces for head and footboards or sides if desired.
5. Stain or paint the bed and lacquer if you like a glossy finish. This bed can also be constructed without using dowels by first gluing the spools together with a strong wood glue.

9. Children's Table and Chair Set

Materials

Sono tube, 4' high, 1' in diameter (can be purchased from a building supply outlet or if you have a friend who works in construction ask him to get one for you).

Plywood 1' x 3½'

9 blocks of wood, 1" x 2"

Screws, glue, shellac, decorator tape, saw, and screwdriver

Stuffing material, e.g. old nylons, shredded paper, or lint from dryer.

These materials will make two chairs and one table.

Method for Chair

1. Make a pattern for a throne chair, 2' high with seat 10" from ground, on newspaper or brown paper. Tape pattern to the sono tube or draw the outline of the chair on the tube and cut out the shape with a saw.
2. Screw 3 blocks for seat supports 1" below seat level and an equal distance apart on the inside of the tube.
3. Cut circle 1' in diameter from the plywood for the seat.
4. Fit seat over the blocks and glue into place.
5. Cover chair with a collage of pictures cut from magazines or use old wallpaper.
6. Glue pictures or wallpaper to chair and cover with a coat of shellac for protection.
7. Bind edges of chair with decorator tape.
8. Make a cushion for the seat from old material and stuff with nylons, shredded newspaper, etc.
9. Invert the pattern for the second chair on the sono tube so enough material will be left to make the table.

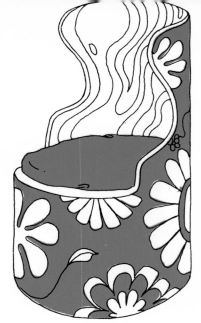

Method for Table

1. After the two chairs have been cut from the sono tube cut the remainder of the tube in a 1' high section.
2. Screw blocks for table top support inside tube at the edges.
3. Cut circle from plywood 1½" in diameter for the table top.
4. Glue the top into place.
5. Decorate the table top with pictures or paint.
6. Bind the edges of the table with tape to match the chairs.

10. Rhythm Band Instruments

A. Maraca
Materials

Plastic bottle, about 24 fl. oz. (such as vinegar bottle)
Rice or dried beans
Scraps of yarn, colored tape, Magic Markers

Method
1. Put about ½ cup rice or dried beans into the bottle and replace cap.
2. Seal lid with decorator tape.
3. Decorate with colored tape or draw a design with a Magic Marker.
4. Make a tassel from unravelled sweater yarn and fasten to the handle.

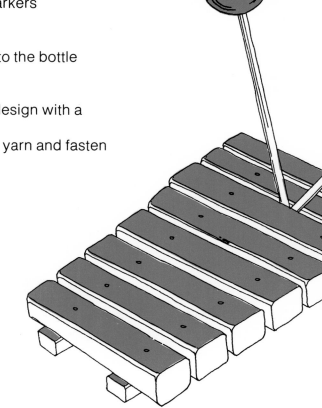

B. Xylophone
Materials

2 hockey stick handles
1″ nails
28″ of cord
Drill, hammer and saw
Wooden or rubber ball, 1″ or 1½″ in diameter
Dowel, Tinker-Toy spindle or pencil

Method
1. Saw a 15″ section from a hockey-stick handle.
2. Saw off 7 more sections, each one ½″ shorter than the one before.
3. Drill a hole 1″ from each end of each section, using a drill bore slightly larger than your nail size.
4. Cut 2 more sections 14″ long to serve as supports.
5. Cut 2 14″ pieces of cord and lay them down the middle of support sections. Fasten the cord at each end with tacks or nails.

6. Loosely nail the graduated sections to the support, resting them on the cord. It is important to nail the sections loosely so that the sections will vibrate when struck.
7. Insert the dowel, spindle or pencil into the ball to form the mallet.
8. Strike the "keys" or sections lightly with the mallet. If the note is off-key, whittle wood away from the underside of the section until the note strikes truly.

C. Drum
Materials

Large plastic bucket such as potato chip or fried chicken bucket
Tape
2' or 3' heavy cord

Method
1. Punch holes for cord in each side of bucket about 1" from top.
2. String cord through and either tie together or knot at each side.
3. Replace lid and seal with tape.
4. Decorate with colored tape.
5. Use wooden spoon handles for drum sticks. The drum can be hung around the child's neck by the cord so he or she can march while drumming.

D. Bongo Drums
Materials

> 1 large (1 gal.) and 1 medium (1 qt.) plastic ice-cream
> bucket

Method
1. Place together, sides touching, and punch 2 sets of small holes opposite each other in each bucket.
2. Fasten the drums together with spread tacks inserted through punch holes.
3. Replace lids and seal shut with tape.
4. Decorate.

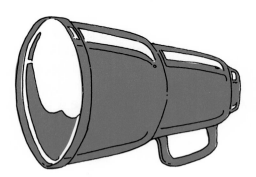

E. Horn or Megaphone
Materials

> Large plastic (gal. size) vinegar or bleach jug with
> handle
> Decorator tape

Method
1. Cut off top of jug right below the screw cap. Cut off the bottom of the jug.
2. Bind mouth edge and bottom edge with tape if you wish.
3. Decorate with Magic Marker or with more tape. Children can sing or shout through this horn and will thoroughly enjoy the sound of their own voices.

Hint

> This instrument makes a good megaphone for calling
> stray kids home for supper, and will save your sanity
> as well as your voice at birthday parties or if you work
> with small fry in groups such as cubs.

F.   Musical Bottles
Materials

> 8 assorted sizes of glass bottles
> Water
> Spoon

Method

1.   Add water to the bottles, testing for sound by tapping bottle with a spoon.
2.   Adjust the water level to obtain the notes of the octave.
3.   When you are satisfied with the sounds, mark the water level in the bottles with a Magic Marker so you can maintain the level as water evaporates. A similar effect can be accomplished by blowing across the mouth of the bottles instead of striking the glass to obtain the note. This is an inexpensive way to give small children an early musical education as they learn to play tunes encompassing the 8-note scale.

G.   Whistle
Materials

> Plastic drinking straw
> Scissors

Method

1.   Cut top of straw to a point and flatten.
2.   Cut 4 holes in the top side of the straw for fingers. Try, and test for hole positions, as no two straws are exactly alike.

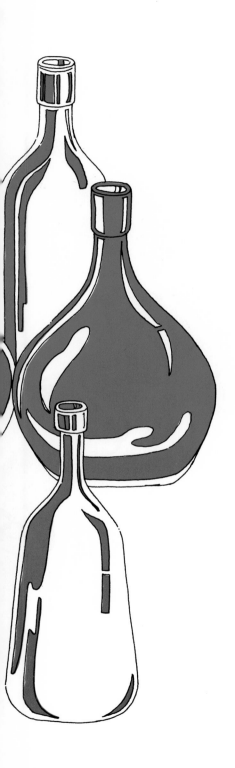

H. Castanets
Materials

4 bottle caps
Board or stick about 6″ x 1″ x ½″
3 nails (one spike and 2 smaller)

Method
1. Take plastic liner out of bottle caps.
2. Using spike, put a hole in centre of each cap.
3. With smaller nail, loosely nail 2 caps back to back at one end of board.
4. Nail 2 more caps just below first set, in a similar way. When the castanets are banged against the palm they will rattle.

I. Rasp
Materials

8 or 10 bottle caps
Block of wood about 4″ x 6″

Method
1. Nail caps to the block, rough side up. Scrape rhythmically with a spoon.

Hint
Rasps or calypso scrapers can also be made by cutting slits in the side of a plastic jug or even in a cardboard tube and scraping with a spike nail. The elbow section from a dryer vent, or any other piece of junk with ridges, will serve the same purpose.

Bell
Materials

Tin can
Nut and screw eye
Cord or pliable wire
6″ of dowel or broom handle

Method
1. Punch hole with a nail in the top of the can.
2. Put screw eye through hole with eye to inside.
3. Screw into dowel which will form handle.
4. Tie or wire a nut or washer to the screw eye to act as dinger. Ring like a cow bell.

11. Clowns

A. Spool Clown
Materials

> 3 large and 18 small thread spools
> 3 ft. of strong cord or pliable wire
> 5 buttons
> Scraps of fabric
> Magic Marker

Method
1. Use 2 strands of cord or wire and thread them through the spools as illustrated.
2. Fasten with a button as an anchor, at the head and end of each limb.
3. Paint on a face and costume with Magic Marker or glue on bits of felt or other fabric.

FINISH

START

B. Cloth Clown
Materials

Colorful cloth scraps
3′ of strong thread or elastic thread
Buttons or bells
Cotton batting or nylon stocking
Embroidery thread

Method

1. Cut 12 cloth circles 1½″ in diameter for each arm and leg, 48 in total, and 14 cloth circles 2″ in diameter for body, from various colored fabrics.
2. Run a draw thread around the circumference of each cirlce about ¼″ from the edge, pull it tight and tie to secure the thread. Flatten by hand or with an iron. This forms the discs for the clown's arms, legs and body.
3. To construct the head, make a tube about 3″ long and 1½″ in diameter from a knit fabric such as underwear.
4. Make a pointed hat from colored material and sew to head.
5. Stuff combined head and hat with cotton batting or shredded nylon stocking.
6. Embroider on a face.
7. Using very strong thread or elastic thread string the discs of cloth the same way spools are strung for spool clown.
8. Use buttons or bells as anchors. If elastic thread and bells are used the clown will bounce and jingle if strung up across baby's crib.

12. Games

A. Ring Toss
Materials

> Wine bottle
> Sand
> A variety of round plastic bottles with different
>   diameters
> Knife

Method
1. Fill a long-necked wine bottle with sand to give it weight so it won't tip.
2. Cut rings from the plastic bottles making them about 1″ deep.
3. Mark 1 point value on large rings, 5 on medium rings and 10 on small, using a Magic Marker or nail polish. Play by tossing the rings over neck of bottle and marking score.

B. Small Fry Golf
Materials

> 4, 1-lb. coffee tins, plus their plastic lids
> Wooden stake, 2′ long
> Styrofoam chunk from packaging
> Ping-pong ball
> Epoxy glue
> Masking tape

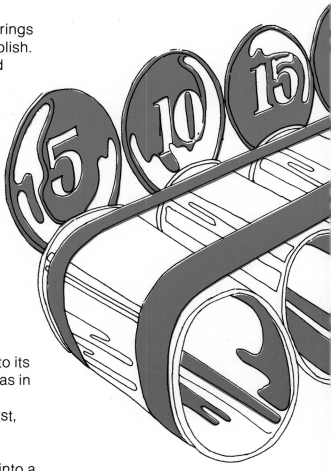

Method
1. Lay each empty can on its side and tape the lid to its bottom so that half the lid shows above the can as in illustration.
2. Using Magic Marker number the lids, 5 on the first, then 10, 15 and 20 on the 3 remaining.
3. Glue the cans together side by side in a line.
4. Make a mallet to hit the ball, by jamming a stick into a piece of styrofoam which has been cut to form a 3″ x 3″ block. Hit the ball into the cans from about 6′ back, keeping score.

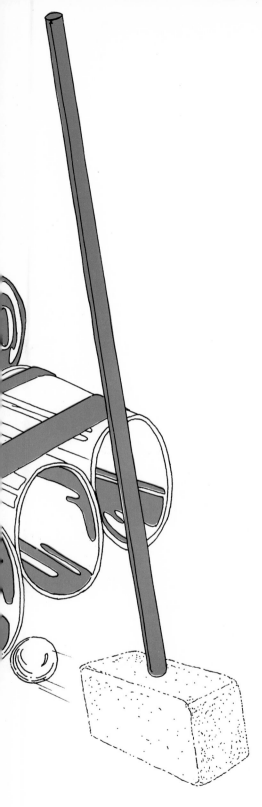

C. Bottle and Clothes-Peg Game
Materials

Bottle with mouth about 2″ wide
Clothes pegs

Method
1. Straddle bottle, and holding pegs at chin level, drop them head first into the bottle. Keep score to see how many pegs you can put in the bottle.

D. Bowling
Materials

6 plastic bottles such as the type used for dish detergent
Sand
Balls

Method
1. Put about 1″ of sand in bottle and replace top. This will weigh down the bottles so they won't tip too easily.
2. Line up bottles in bowling position. Bowl with sponge balls, or balls carved from styrofoam packing.

E. Stocking Games
Materials

Nylon stocking
Rubber ball

Method
1. Put a rubber ball in the toe of old stocking and bounce it side to side against the wall: "One, two, three, O'Leary."
2. Use same ball and stocking for one arm skipping. Swing it low around legs skipping over as it spins.
3. Nylon stocking can be a sling shot. Fold in half, toe to top. Place ball in pocket of the fold. Twirl over head and let fly well out of reach of windows or there will be broken glass to recycle.

13. Dolls

A. Sock Doll
Materials

Odd work socks
Embroidery thread
Old nylons
Unravelled wool or yarn pieces
Scissors, needle and thread

Method

1. Cut the foot off a sock stopping before curve of heel. Using only the toe of the sock, stuff with a nylon stocking for the head of the doll. Using yarn, draw tightly and tie to form the ball head. If you are making a boy doll you can tie the yarn into a bow to make a bow tie.
2. Starting at cut edge, slit front and back of sock for 3" to form legs.
3. Stuff the doll body with more nylons.
4. Stitch around the inside of legs and crotch, stuff legs and stitch to close at the feet.
5. Using another portion of the sock, make arms by forming two tubes 1½" long and 1" wide. Stuff and sew arms to the body.
6. Tie yarn tightly at the wrists to form hands and make the feet in the same way.
7. Stitch a face on the doll with yarn or embroidery thread.
8. To make the doll's hat, cut the sock cuff, 3" from the top. Draw the raw edge to a point and whipstitch to secure the edge.
9. Stitch the hat to the doll's head and roll back finished edge to form a toque. If you want a girl doll use the cuff cut off 3" from the top for a skirt by placing cuff wrong side up around the doll's waist, and stitching to waist. Turn down to form skirt. Make long hair or braids from scraps of yarn and stitch to head. A small hat can be made for the girl doll by using bits from other sections of the sock, and stitching them to the head.

B.   Character Doll
Materials

Scraps of fabric

Nylon stockings (or lint from the dryer)

Scraps of old clothing from the person the doll is portraying

Props (toy guitar, fountain pen or any object typifying the person the doll is caricaturing)

Method

1. Trace the whole shape of the body of the doll on paper, exaggerating the features that identify the person such as big muscles, large feet, potbelly, etc.
2. Using the tracing as a pattern, cut two pieces of fabric for the body.
3. Again, using the tracing as a pattern, cut the clothing for the doll—jacket, pants, dress.
4. Sew around the edges of the fabric used for the body, leaving an opening for the stuffing.
5. Repeat the same method for the clothing.
6. Turn the fabric for the doll's body and the clothing right side out.
7. Dress the empty doll with the clothing and then stuff the doll. The clothes will fit tightly on the doll when this method is used.
8. Embroider facial features on the doll.
9. Make hair from loops of fabric or yarn. The hair is often a distinguishing characteristic and can be emphasized.
10. Use your imagination and emphasize doll's bosom or make a hairy chest. Add props such as horn for a musician, skis, glasses, etc. These dolls are marvellous to give as gifts especially when they have been fashioned to resemble the recipient. Children love to see material used for the doll's clothes from their own well-loved but worn-out clothing. It makes the doll very "special" and very much their own.

Hint

Even when using a commercial pattern for a stuffed toy such as the dog pictured on page 4, use old materials from children's outworn garments.
It makes the toy more personal and nylon stuffing makes toy machine washable and easy to dry.

14. Masks

Materials
Nylon stocking

Method
1. The perfect Halloween mask can be made from the top half of a nylon stocking. The greatest advantage to this mask is its safety; it does not impair vision, hearing or breathing. Pull stocking down over head. The age, sex and appearance of the wearer become unrecognizable. A completely new face can be made by pulling up on the stocking; this raises the facial features and slants the eyes. The stocking makes a mask which will fit an adult or child.

Hint
Braided nylons make good "pin-on" pigtalls, as well as tails for donkeys, etc. They dye well with commercial home dye. Shell out!

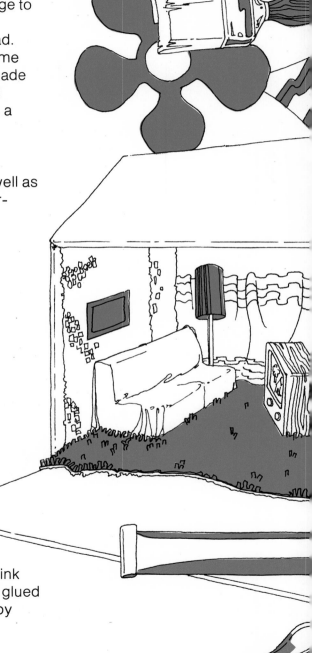

15. Simple Dollhouse for a Child to Make

Materials
Heavy corrugated boxes
Scraps of wallpaper
Cloth
Paint
Rug scraps
Linoleum scraps
Knife
Glue
Magazine pictures

Method
1. Arrange boxes on side in order and shape you think most suitable for your house. For example, three glued side by side for a ranchstyle bungalow or 2 side by side and two more on top for a 4-room, 2-storey house.

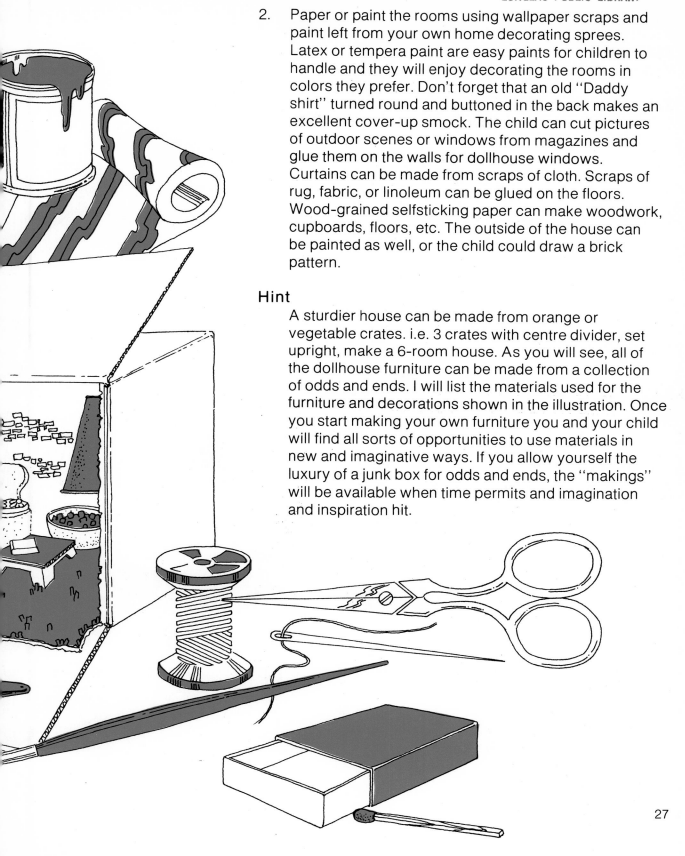

2. Paper or paint the rooms using wallpaper scraps and paint left from your own home decorating sprees. Latex or tempera paint are easy paints for children to handle and they will enjoy decorating the rooms in colors they prefer. Don't forget that an old "Daddy shirt" turned round and buttoned in the back makes an excellent cover-up smock. The child can cut pictures of outdoor scenes or windows from magazines and glue them on the walls for dollhouse windows. Curtains can be made from scraps of cloth. Scraps of rug, fabric, or linoleum can be glued on the floors. Wood-grained selfsticking paper can make woodwork, cupboards, floors, etc. The outside of the house can be painted as well, or the child could draw a brick pattern.

Hint

A sturdier house can be made from orange or vegetable crates. i.e. 3 crates with centre divider, set upright, make a 6-room house. As you will see, all of the dollhouse furniture can be made from a collection of odds and ends. I will list the materials used for the furniture and decorations shown in the illustration. Once you start making your own furniture you and your child will find all sorts of opportunities to use materials in new and imaginative ways. If you allow yourself the luxury of a junk box for odds and ends, the "makings" will be available when time permits and imagination and inspiration hit.

16. Dollhouse Furniture

Materials

Bedroom:

    Bed—foam rubber covered with piece of dress material.

    End table—matchbox cut and glued together.

    Swag lamp—lid from aerosol can and chain.

    Pictures—slide holders and snapshots.

    Vanity—tin cans, cardboard, fabric.

    Stool—spool.

    Mirror—tin-can lid.

    Lamps—flash bulbs and pill-bottle caps.

    TV—flashcube and creamer.

Nursery:

    Bassinet—detergent bottle and wool.

    Lamps and table—spray-can and detergent-bottle cap.

    Play pen—berry box.

    Balls—beads.

    Dresser—small matchboxes.

    Shelf—paper clips and popsicle stick.

    Rocking chair—egg carton.

Kitchen:

Windows—magazine pictures.

Table—cheese box and deodorant block stand.

Chairs—toilet rolls and foam rubber.

Divider—berry box, creamers, parts cut from artificial flower arrangements.

Counter and sink—egg carton.

Taps—screw.

Stove—buttons.

Refrigerator—baby-powder can.

Cupboards—cereal boxes.

Bird cage—plastic mesh container for water softener for dishwashers.

Towel rod—Tin-can zip-top.

Living Room:

Hanging chair—half of an egg-shaped plastic stocking container, and chain.

Paintings—magazine pictures.

Table and plant—deodorant block container, creamer and piece of an artificial plant.

Tapestry—strip of fabric.

Chairs—calendar tube, foam and pyjama fabric.

Coffee table—pill box and popsicle sticks.

Books—match books.

Vase—bottle cap

Fireplace—string cone, plastic stocking container, beans, yoghurt lid and aquarium sand.

TV—slide container and snapshot.

Speakers—candy paper.

Candle and holder—birthday candle and nut.

Lamps—fuse and toilet roll, curtain hook, pencil and spool.

Couch—foam chunk from pillow and pyjama material.

Hints

Book shelves, a play pen and fences can be made with popsicle sticks. Fixtures, people, pets, etc., can be modelled with play dough. (See the recipe for play dough on **page 30**) Styrofoam egg cartons carve very easily and can be used for counter tops, fixtures, etc. Try making furniture from cereal boxes, drawers from match boxes, and books from match packs.

29

17. Sailboat

Materials
    2 styrofoam meat trays, about 4" x 6"
    Stick or scrap wire
    Divider from egg cartons

Method
1. Cut the egg carton divider into a 4" piece and glue to centre of styrofoam tray.
2. Cut 3" x 5" sail from second tray.
3. Poke wire or popsicle stick through sail and also into divider. Presto, a dandy boat for bathtub cruising.

18. Punching Bag

Materials
    Newspapers
    Rope

Method
1. Make a very large roll of newspapers, about 1' in diameter.
2. Bind securely with rope.
3. Hang from a tree or beam in basement and take out your frustrations on it.

19. Play Dough

Materials
    3 cups of flour
    1 cup of salt
    4 tbsp. of cooking oil
    1 cup of water
    Food coloring added to water if desired

Method
1. Blend all ingredients together. If more malleable dough is desired add more water.
2. Keep in airtight containers.

20. Papier-mâché

Method
1. Tear newspapers into ½″ x 3″ strips if you are going to work on fine objects. For larger objects use larger strips of paper.
2. Dip newspaper strips into a solution of wallpaper paste mixed to the consistency of pea soup.
3. The wet strips are then moulded over the frame or shape desired for each object. It can be used to cover tin cans, jars or plastic containers (see candle holders in chapter VII, page 84). Jewellery can also be made from papier-mâché as well as puppets, dolls, etc.

Hint
If papier-mâché is put into a blender and mulched finely, it can be used to mould shapes in the same way asbestos or clay is used.

21. Nylons—Tips for Kids

Kindergarten Teacher's Pet
Slip nylons over tots' shoes to help them slide into those tight boots.
Pull the nylon up over pant legs and it will help keep them tucked inside the boots. Nylons also make good shoe protectors inside galoshes for adults' suede or fancy shoes.

Bandage or Cast Slipcover
A nylon slipped over bandages will help keep them clean and protect them from unravelling yet allow ventilation. Similarly, they can be used over a cast to keep it clean. A stocking around neck and arm cast also makes a good sling.

iii kitchen tools, tips and gadgets

1. Funnel

Materials
Plastic bottle, small 24-oz. vinegar-bottle size

Method
1. Remove lid.
2. Cut off neck and upper part of the bottle to make funnel.
3. Invert the neck and presto, a funnel to help you when pouring liquid into small-mouthed containers.
4. You can make a variety of funnels to meet individual needs from different sizes of plastic bottles.

2. Chopping Can

Materials
Tin can, 10-oz. size

Method
1. Cut the can so that it is left with a sharp edge. (Cans that open with a key have a ready-made sharp edge.)
2. Punch holes in the closed end with a nail or ice pick. These holes give air an escape route. This amazing invention is good for chopping cold potatoes, beets, etc., and can do just as good a job as the expensive commercial choppers.

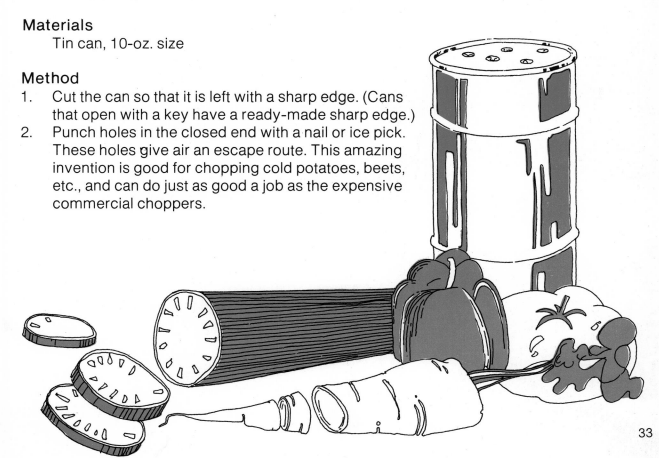

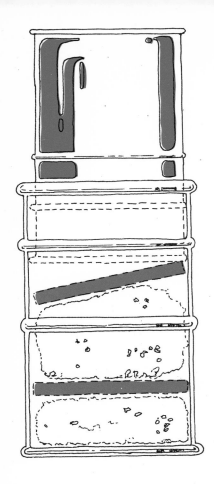

3. Patty Stacker

Materials
1 10-oz. soup can
1 14-15 oz. can
Styrofoam meat trays

Method
1. Cut both top and bottom from the larger of the two cans.
2. Remove lid only from the smaller can.
3. Cut round discs from the styrofoam meat trays, sized to fit inside the larger can.
4. Take one portion of hamburger and insert it into the large can on your chopping board.
5. Place a disc over hamburger, then insert small can and using the second can as a packer, press down.
6. Continue to add hamburger and discs and press until you have a column of hamburgers.
7. Lift the can and remove the stack from the bottom. The patties can be used immediately or wrapped and frozen for future use. The discs make it easy to separate the patties.

4. Strainer

Materials
Old nylon stocking, washed and boiled to sterilize

Method
1. A section of old nylon can be stretched over the mouth of a container and used as a strainer.
   Examples:
   A. to remove skin from left over paint.
   B. to remove skin of mould from syrup.
   C. As a jelly bag for preserving fruit juice or jelly. Pour cooked fruit into stocking and hang while juice drips through. To do this use the stocking intact and hang from top.

5. Loaf Pans

Materials
Tin cans, 10-oz. size

Method
1. Round loaves of fruit bread or Christmas fruit puddings bake very well in buttered tin cans. Cut out end with can opener to remove loaf or pudding and just push it through. Wash can, flatten and see that it gets to the recycling depot.

6. Measuring Scoops

Materials
Small plastic bottles
Scissors or kitchen knife

Method
1. Cut bottles into scoop shapes with knife.
2. Try filling scoops from your measuring cup and mark the level with a Magic Marker: ½, ¼, ⅓ and 1 cup. These are useful to measure sugar, flour, etc.

7. Tote for Cleaning Products

Materials
Plastic jug, about 1 gal. size
10" heavy cord

Method
1. Cut neck off the plastic jug, leaving a shape like a bucket.
2. Punch hole on each side and insert cord for handle. This can be carried on your belt or just transported from room to room while cleaning and is a light and effective tote for carrying wet rags or spillable products.

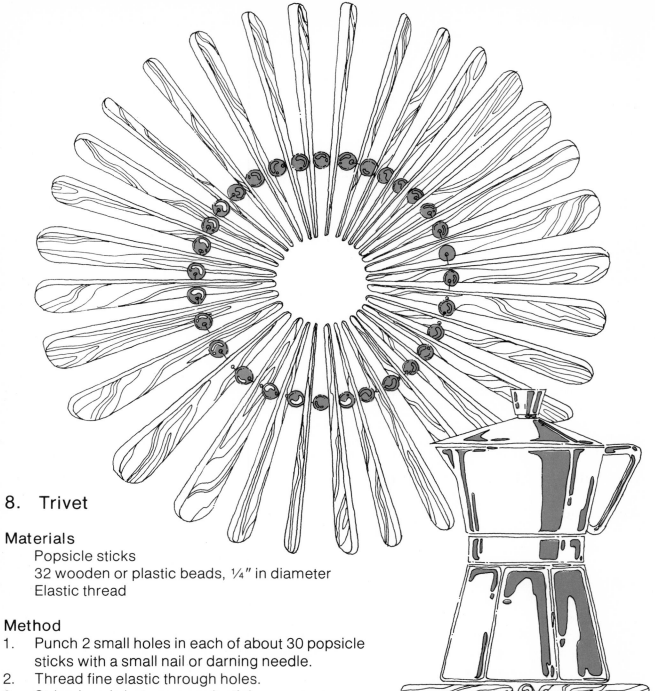

8. Trivet

Materials
Popsicle sticks
32 wooden or plastic beads, ¼″ in diameter
Elastic thread

Method
1. Punch 2 small holes in each of about 30 popsicle sticks with a small nail or darning needle.
2. Thread fine elastic through holes.
3. String beads between each stick as spacers.
4. Bottom elastic is drawn tight and tied. Tie other elastics graduating the tension. Trivet will spread into a circle.
5. Placed under hot plates or casserole dishes, this trivet will protect your table or counter from scorches.

9. Hot Mats to Protect Table or Counter

Materials
6 pr. of old nylon stockings, or scrap material

Method
1. Cut scrap material into strips 1½″ wide. If you are using nylons, cut off the feet and thick upper section and braid. You can dye them to match your color scheme.
2. Braid the strips together. As you end one piece, sew on another and continue to braid.
3. Sew or lace braid into a coil, using heavy thread. The mat will be about 10″ in diameter.

Hint
Nylons can also be knitted or crocheted into mats. Although nylon mats work well under warm or reasonably hot pans, very hot pans should be placed on mats made from wool or cotton.

10. Dish Cloths and Dusters

If you are an addicted string saver, knit or crochet it into dish cloths. Use a garter stitch. The number of stitches and size of needle will determine the size and lightness of your cloth. These will be machine washable, and will wear longer than sponges or commercial synthetic cloths.

11. Cleaning Cloths
Old bath towels or other absorbent materials make excellent cleaning cloths. Who needs commercial cloths or sponges when these will do an equal job? Old newspapers dampened in vinegar and water, clean mirrors and windows just as well as disposable paper towels and costly commercial window-cleaning products.

12. Pet Dishes

Materials
Plastic bottles, 64-oz. or 1 gal. jug size
Knife
Paint or Magic Marker

Method
1. Cut plastic jugs about 2″ from bottom. Put the tops away for a future project. i.e. scoop or megaphone.
2. Decorate with names, etc. with Magic Markers or paint. These dishes don't chip or break and are easily cleaned. If Fido decides to chew his dish, then just start with another bottle and no cost is involved.

Hint
These bottle bottoms also make good saucers under potted plants, or dishes for young campers—the taller 10-oz. size makes a handy unbreakable tumbler and the 48-oz. size makes a good cereal bowl.

13. Jardiniere

Materials
Plastic bottle
Paint, Magic Markers, decorating tape

Method
1. Cut neck from bottle and use the remainder of the bottle to hold a flower pot.
2. Decorate with paint, etc. It can be hung with cord or rope macrame or nylons cut in spirals and dyed an attractive color. (This method of cutting nylons prevents running and the raw edges curl to the inside.) These plant holders are waterproof and won't scratch the surface of the sill.

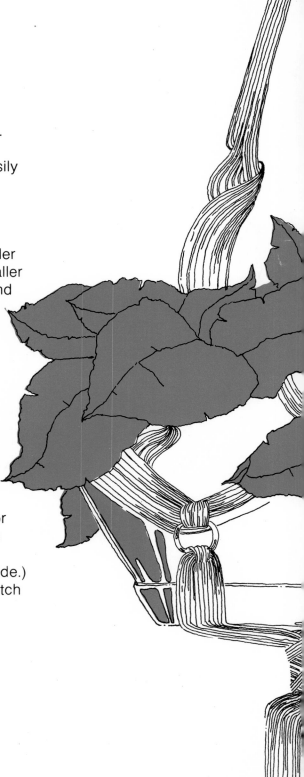

14. Recipe Holder

Materials

Disposable plastic fork and creamer as used in snack bars

Plasticine or play dough

Method

1. Put dab of plasticine or play dough (see page 30) in the bottom of a creamer.
2. Press handle of plastic fork into the dough before it hardens and smooth it around handle. Your recipe fits in the tines of the fork. The little trough around the handle could hold toothpicks for testing cakes, or sprigs of home-grown herbs for seasoning.

Hint

For another variation on the same idea, instead of a creamer, substitute a small pot of parsley or herbs and insert a swizzle stick into soil, prongs up, to hold recipe. Of course you ecology-minded people will avoid using disposable cutlery, cups and creamers wherever possible.

15. Place Mats

Materials

Brown paper bags

Method

1. Open out bags and cut into strips 4" wide and 14" long.
2. Fold strips 3 times to make final strips 1" wide and 4 layers thick. Make 6 strips with this method.
3. Glue shut.
4. Make 8 more strips 12" long, using same method.
5. Weave short strips up and down and long strips back and forth in basket weave.
6. Press strips close together and glue ends to hold.
7. Trim edges neatly.
8. Paint to suit your color scheme or leave plain.
9. Mats can be shellacked to make them more resistant to spills.

16. Kitchen Hints for Recyclers

Glass, Jars and Bottles

Your imagination should start working as soon as a bottle or jar comes into the house. A simple glass cutter found on your favorite Boy Scout's jack-knife, or purchased at a hardware store, can turn a glass jar or bottle into a very respectable drinking glass. Heavy sandpaper or pumice rubbed around the cut edge will look after any sharp edges. Wine bottles and many other bottles with varied colors and shapes, such as syrup and juice bottles, are pretty as flower containers in their own right. The homebrew-wine master will be happy to receive any old wine bottles or reasonable facsimiles you have saved. You will, of course, remember to lay away a good supply of jars till the jelly and pickle season, and in the meantime, they make good refrigerator storage jars.

17. Leftovers

Budget-conscious cooks hate waste and enjoy a challenge. Here are a few suggestions for things to do with leftover food instead of putting it into the garbage.

1. Don't throw away sour milk just because the kids say "yuk". Use it in cake, muffin or fruit bread recipes or in any recipe that calls for buttermilk.
2. Stale bread can be made into croutons for homemade soup or tossed salads by cutting it into cubes and frying in oil or butter with garlic salt. Or it can be dried in oven, and crushed into crumbs for casserole toppings. Or kept in a plastic bag in the fridge or freezer for a dressing for fowl, fish or chops.
3. Drippings can be saved and used in many recipes in place of oil or lard. (Use carefully for family members with high cholesterol counts.) Drippings added daily to your dog or cat's dinner will give him (or her) a glossy coat and aid regularity. Birds enjoy drippings almost as much as suet—pour drippings into a shallow tin can or plastic container, let it harden, and put it on your bird-feeding station, or put chunks in a mesh onion bag and hang from a tree. Woodpeckers will love this.

4. Dried orange peels make a fragrant kindling for fire starters. Tangerines and juice orange peelings are particularly good as they are easier to dehydrate without moulding. Grapefruit, lemon or orange peels can also be candied. They make a tart but sweet confection. Or you can pulverize the dried peels in your blender to use for flavoring in your baking.

5. If there is enough food left over for a couple of servings after dinner, place the portions on tinfoil plates. Wrap the plates tightly with foil and freeze. These will come in handy if someone is eating at an odd hour of if you feel just plain lazy. These dinners also make a good gift for someone living alone who wouldn't find it convenient to cook a roast or casserole for themselves. Your pets will enjoy a TV dinner too. If the cook goofed and there are more plate scrapings than your dog or cat can handle in one meal, wrap it up and freeze for a future meal. Vets highly recommend table scraps as a pet food supplement, because they contain the nutrients necessary for healthy animals.

6. If you simply can't think of any way to make your garbage adaptable, then compost the raw vegetables, fruit and egg shells. This makes a rich organic fertilizer which can be used on lawns, flower beds or vegetable gardens where it will come back to you again in the next cycle of food. See method on **page 56**

iv garden and garage gadgets

1. Bird Houses

A. Tin-Can Wren House
Materials
Coffee tin with plastic cap
Kitchen knife
Ice pick
1 coat hanger

Method
1. Cut hole in plastic cap about 1″ in diameter and about ⅔ of the way from the bottom. For some reason known only to Jenny Wren these are the preferred measurements for her dream home.
2. Insert a small stick about ½″ under hole for a perch.
3. Punch hole in upper edge of plastic cap and another in upper edge of can bottom with a nail or ice pick and thread straightened coat hanger through the two punched holes.
4. Bend hanger up from edge of can and join. Hook on hanger can be bent to hook over a branch.
5. The metal can and hanger should be sprayed with rust-resistant paint, preferably with a mat finish, as shiny objects may frighten away birds. You can glue strips of cedar bark on the surface of the tin if you want a more natural appearance for your bird house.
6. House should be hung 8′ to 10′ above ground (again by special request of wren families). The plastic cap can be snapped off for cleaning at the end of the season.

B. Milk-Carton House
Materials

> 1 qt. milk carton
> Coat hanger or cord
> Tape

Method
1. Clean carton and close top opening with masking tape.
2. Cut hole similar to method in A.
3. Hanger or cord can be threaded under peaked roof and used to hang house.

C. Plastic Jug House
Materials

> Plastic jug with side handle, 64-oz. size
> Nylon stocking

Method
1. Cut hole in side of jug about 6″ from bottom, and about 1″ in diameter.
2. Make perch as in A.
3. Use strong, weather-resistant nylon to lash jug handle to tree branch. Apartment dwellers can fasten their bird house to a balcony railing instead of a tree branch.
4. Choose a jug with a subdued color or paint it a dark shade. Birds are wary of bright colors or shiny surfaces.

D. Wooden Birdhouse or Robin Shelter
Materials

> Wood from old packing crates or boxes
> Nails

Method
1. A regular birdhouse or robin shelter with open sides can be made using the wood from old crates or baskets. Nail boards together to form floor and two sides.
2. Put sloping roof on top to overhang floor or shelter.
3. Hang about 10 ft. from ground on a wall near trees and away from doorways or other traffic areas.

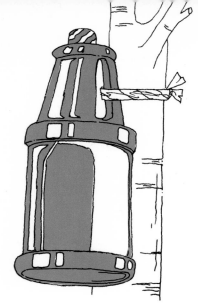

2. Bird Feeders

A. Plastic-Bottle Feeder
Materials

Plastic bottle, 64-oz. size, with side handle
Kitchen knife

Method
1. Cut sides from bottle as shown in picture.
2. Lash to a branch by wrapping a nylon stocking through handle and around the branch. This type of feeder can be hung from a window frame or veranda railing, and it's just the thing for apartment dwellers.

B. Self-Replenishing Bird Feeder
Materials

2 plastic jugs, 64-oz. detergent size
Kitchen knife
Tape
Cord

Method
1. Cut the jug as shown.
2. Cut away neck and upper half of small bottle and fit it into large jug so that the wide end is in jug neck and narrow end is about ½″ from floor of the jug.
3. Tape into position.
4. Fill inner bottle with bird seed through neck of jug and replace cap. The seeds will drop as the birds eat.
5. Lash to a tree or railing or hang with strong cord or nylon stocking.

Hint

A bird tray can be hung outside any window including those in the highest apartments. Birds like the fat cut from meat or meat dripping almost as well as suet. A section of log can be hung up and fat spread into the bark for birds to feed upon.

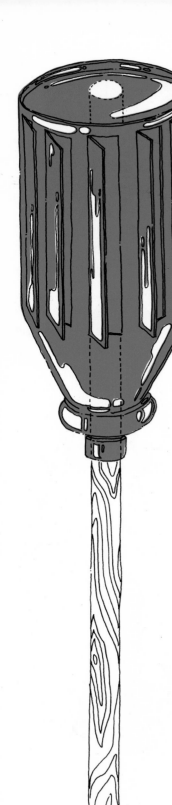

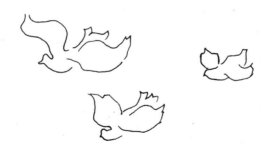

3. Bird "Shooer"
Materials

Plastic bottle (must be round)
Wooden stake or broom handle
Kitchen knife

Method
1. Make slits in bottle as shown in diagram.
2. Make vertical cuts starting about 1″ from top and finishing about 1″ from bottom of jug. Make 1″ cuts from each slit going horizontally, top and bottom.
3. Score from edge of each slit and bend outward far enough so that the wind will catch these flaps.
4. Cut a hole in bottom of jug larger than stake and insert stake right up into the neck of the bottle. The bottle should spin freely on the stake.
5. Stick these "shooers" in garden and berry patch. The breeze will cause them to spin, frightening away the feathered robbers. Of course you could always resort to the old scarecrow and recycle a few choice articles of old clothing for his costume.

4. Patio Lanterns

A. Japanese Lantern

Materials

Plastic bottle, about 64-oz. size (Wisk and Fleecy
   come in pretty red and blue plastic)
8″ cord
Sharp kitchen knife
Short candle stub
Small tin can or lid

Method

1. Cut top off the plastic bottle with a knife. Using lower portion, make vertical slits about 1″ apart with sharp knife, stopping 1″ from top and stopping 1″ from bottom, leaving about 1″ uncut top and bottom.
2. Score each strip across the middle and press down to make slits stay open.
3. Make heavy knots in both ends of a 1½′ cord. Put knots through slits on opposite sides to form handle.
4. Fasten small tin can or tin lid in the bottom of the bottle with a spread tack.
5. Stick on candle with a little melted wax. The can will catch candle drips and will prevent the plastic from melting if the candle should tip over.
6. Hang from a tree or veranda roof.

Hint

With this same method either with or without the cuts you can make a good hanging jardinier for inside or out-of-doors. For this purpose, hang cords from 3 points: Punch 3 holes spaced an equal distance apart and insert 3 cords. Join cords and hang from spot of intersection. These containers can be used in place of ceramic pots in a macrame hanging. I have also used coffee cups or mugs which have had the handles knocked off as hanging jardiniers.

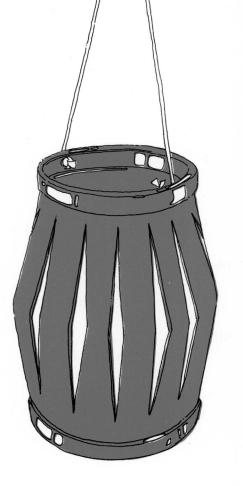

B. Mexican Lantern
Materials

Coffee or nut tin, preferably one without ridges
Screwdriver or chisel
Hammer

Method
1. Fill can with water and freeze until it becomes a block of ice. This gives you a solid core to work against so the can won't dent. Work quickly before melting begins.
2. Use the chisel or differently shaped screwdrivers as your tools to hammer holes into a design on the can.
3. Melt the ice and dry.
4. Paint a suitable color or leave plain.
5. Fasten small candle in centre with melted wax. These are marvellous lanterns for a picnic table or hung outdoors as patio lamps.

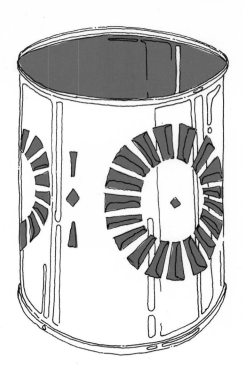

5. Barbecue Fire Starter

Materials
48-oz. juice can
Triangular can punch

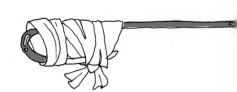

Method
1. Cut out both ends of can.
2. Use a triangular can punch and punch all around one end at base working from the inside and letting cut-away pieces go down to bottom to form legs. It may be necessary to use pliers to pull legs down a little.
3. Set on feet in the barbecue. Place kindling in bottom and fill with charcoal.
4. Light from below. The holes and little feet allow draft to speed burning. After all coals are glowing, lift can with tongs and spread coals out ready for barbecuing.

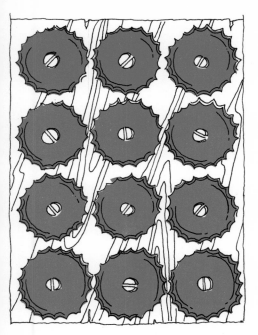

6. Mud Scraper or Fish Scaler

Materials
Block of wood
12 pop or beer-bottle caps
Nails
Hammer

Method
1. Nail caps onto block, ragged side up, driving nail through centre of cap. Block should be about 3"x 4" or a good size for gripping. Use as scraper for muddy boots. It can even be nailed to back step so boots can be scraped farm style. If you have model children who never walk through mud, then use your invention as a fish scaler.

7. Hot Dog or Marshmallow Sticks or Shishkebob Skewers

Materials
Coat hangers
Pliers with wire cutters

Method
1. Cut open coat hanger.
2. Snip off hook and straighten. Wrap one end of skewer with wool fabric scrap for easier grip. It also helps to protect hands from heat. One hanger makes 1 long skewer or 2 short ones if you like toasting your toes as well as your food.

Hint
People are often unaware that the bark of some of our common trees is poisonous and should not be used for hot dog or marshmallow skewers on hiking and camping trips. Even if campers are aware of this fact, trees are sometimes hard to identify in winter, so stay on the safe side and use handy homemade skewers.

8. Jungle Gym

Materials

Old lead pipe 1½" to 2" in diameter. The size of jungle gym you want will determine how many lengths of pipe you need. The best height for cross-bar walking, swinging, "skin-the-cat" and flips, is about 4' from the ground. Allowing for 2' or 3' of pipe to go underground, you would need pipe 6' to 7' long. The cross-bar lengths are your own choice. For a jungle gym to hang from, or for chinning and hand-over-hand exercises, the height of the cross bar from the ground should be 6' or 7'. You would need pipe 8' to 9' long for this type of gym.

Elbows, 2 to a set
Cement (50 lb. bag of ready-mix)
Shovel and pail

Method

1. Assemble pipes, screwing posts and cross bars into pipe elbows.
2. Dig holes 2' or 3' deep, spaced according to your cross-bar lengths. (Make sure to locate the gym far enough away from fences and trees so that kids can jump and tumble without injury.)
3. Stand the assembled pipes into holes, ensuring that the cross bar is level.
4. Find an assistant to hold pipes upright while you pack holes with gravel, stones, earth or for added stability, cement. Tamp earth and stones down or if you are using cement allow it to harden properly before turning the kids loose on the gym.

9. Super Duper Pooper Scooper

Materials

48-oz. plastic bottle with side handle
Knife

Method

1. Cut bottle in a shape that resembles a scoop holding handle toward top. This is a handy yard aid for the pet owner on poo patrol. Take your pooper scooper with you when you are walking your dog in the park. It will keep you and your dog on the good citizen list.

Hint

A similar scoop will come in handy for spreading peat moss, compost in the garden, or even included with a bucket of sand in the car trunk for a slippery winter day.

10. Nylon Stockings for Man's Best Friend

A. Dog Collar Protector

To protect your dog's ruff from staining or cutting from his choker collar, just slip the chain through an old nylon stocking. It will give with the expansion and contraction of the choker action.

B. Dog Collar and Lead

Tie one end of the stocking in a small loop. The remainer of the stocking can pass through the loop and act as a combination choker collar and lead. It makes a very strong collar and lead and will not damage the dog's fur.

C. Dog or Cat Muzzle

Wrap a nylon stocking around animal's snout from top to bottom and back behind the neck where it is tied. The nylon is strong and won't hurt or cut the animal's fur. This is an easy way to restrain a nervous animal for grooming, nail clipping or dressing wounds. It is also a good way to cure excessive barking or a chewy pup. It can be quickly applied and easily released. Fits any size of animal.

11. Plant Collars

Materials
Small plastic ice cream containers
Kitchen knife

Method
1. Cut bottoms out of containers and install around small seedling plants as you put them in the ground. Collar should be under the ground and only surface at top edge. Cut worms only attack your plants (and do just what their name suggest to the root of the seedling) in the first inch or two of soil. They won't go deep enough to pass under the collar so plants, and especially tomatoes, are protected from one of their worst enemies.

12. Plant Starters

Materials
Egg carton
Eggshells
Light soil

Method
1. Fill each section of a styrofoam egg carton with the washed half of an eggshell filled with soil.
2. Plant 3 or 4 seeds in each section.
3. When seedling is big enough, lift out half shell and plant it with the seedling. Shell acts as fertilizer and will decompose in ground.

13. Mini Greenhouse

Materials
Egg cartons cut in half lengthwise.
Eggshells
Plastic berry box
Plastic wrap

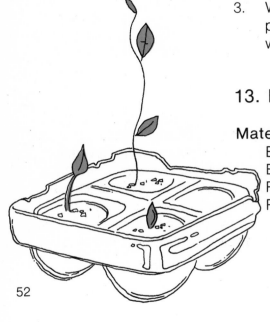

Method
1. Plant seeds as shown in 12.
2. Invert berry box over the egg crate holding seeds and stretch plastic wrap over it.
3. Tend seeds as usual. This acts as a mini greenhouse and speeds growth.

14. Flower Arrangements from Weeds and Dead Plants

Materials
In autumn, pick grasses, grain, dead mullin, milkweed, sunflower heads, dock, goldenrod, teasel, bitter-sweet, straw-flowers, dead zinnias, marigolds and other plants and flowers from your garden or from roadsides. If you look closely, you will see that dead plants and weeds are often very beautiful.

Method
1. Let your garden annuals go to seed on the stalk. Recycle them. Here are 3 steps to follow:
    A. Collect some of the seeds for next year's planting or
    B. Use plants in their dead dry state, in an artistic arrangement.
    C. Compost them.
    Plants may be used just as they are, pruned a little or used as sections, i.e. pods, heads, stalks. The artistic eye can see ways to arrange them as to color, texture and mass. For example, they look charming arranged in an old kitchen pot that might be destined for the garbage, or in a cracked piece of crockery that will no longer hold water. Try mounting them on an old piece of weathered board. The seeds or pods alone can also be glued on burlap to create a wall hanging. You can use pine cones in the same way and save some for your Christmas wreath.

15. Plant Ties

Materials
Old nylon stockings

Method
1. Nothing works better for tying rose bushes, trees, plants, etc. than old nylons. They resist weather, have enough give to them so that they won't injure the plants and are strong, strong, strong.

Hint
When bulbs are taken up for the winter, store them in an old nylon. They will have the ventilation they need and can be hung by nailing to the basement walls or ceiling so the absent-minded gardener won't forget where they are when needed.

16. Workbench File ("File your nails")

Type 1
Materials

Clear plastic jars (16-oz. size is good) with lids. (Some peanut butter is packaged in this type of container.)
Wire or masking tape
Old bicycle wheel

Method
1. Remove tire and clean grease from old wheel with solvent.
2. Prepare your see-through jars by punching 2 holes a couple of inches apart, about 2″ from top, and another set of holes about 2″ from bottom.
3. Thread wire through holes and around spokes of the wheel with tops of the jars facing rim of wheel. Masking tape will serve the purpose if you have no wire.
4. Mount the jars in a circle around the wheel about halfway between rim and hub.
5. Mount the wheel on a peg or spike nail against a wall so that it will turn.
6. Sort your nails, screws, etc., according to size. As you need the different items, turn the wheel so required jar is facing up, then open for easy removal.

7. Colored plastic jars can be used in place of the clear and can be easily labelled for contents with a Magic Marker. You can also wind small lengths of rope or wire around the wheel rim for easy storage.

Type 2
Materials

Glass or plastic jars with screw tops
Nails or screws

Method
1. Nail or screw lids of jars on the underside of the bottom shelf in work area.
2. Screw the jars onto their lids and label according to content if they are not see-through. The hardware will be easily seen and work-shop space is saved for the family "handy person."

Hint
Crates and packing boxes make good garage shelves and cupboards, taken apart or used intact. .

17. Tool Caddy

Materials
Plastic bottle such as the kind with top handle used for oil and antifreeze containers

Method
1. Cut an opening in the container at the top leaving handle intact. Presto! Your tool caddy. This particular size holds hammers, screwdrivers, etc.

18. Bike Rack

Materials
Side removed from old playpen or crib
14' of scrap wood—two by fours
Nails

Method

1. Make a 2' x 5' rectangle frame from the two-by-four scrap wood.
2. Fasten crib or playpen side across the centre of the rectangle, lengthwise.
3. Nail supports to frame and crib side, to hold rack upright. The horizontal base should be about 1' in front of rack and 1' behind.

19. Compost or "Yucky Garbage" Fertilizer

All kitchen garbage that is vegetation i.e. peelings, greens, as well as tea leaves, eggshells, etc. should be saved for composting.

1. Dig a pit about 2' x 4' in a corner of your garden and pile the soil to one side.
2. Make a roof from old boards or plywood etc. to protect the compost heap from direct rain but leaving space for ventilation.
3. Dump in kitchen garbage of fruits and vegetables and sprinkle a little of the soil over it. Repeat. It should be kept slightly moist but not soaking as this will cool the composting action.
4. Turn mixture of soil and garbage by digging it over, about once a week.
5. Prepared chemicals can be purchased to speed the action but it will break down by itself in about 2 months. This compost will make a rich organic fertilizer and can be used throughout the garden.
6. Grass clippings, leaves and plant trimmings make a compost also, but at a slower rate. A separate pile should be made for this type of compost.

20. Ecological Tips for Gardeners

A. If you like the heavy-duty phosphate detergents for your laundry, pollution-minded people can use it with a free conscience for a gardening aid. Keep a bucket of this type of detergent solution for overnight soaking of super soiled clothes. Later wring out clothes and wash in no-phosphate detergent or soap. Your pail of dirty phosphate detergent can be used to sprinkle over your compost heap. The same chemical is present in these detergents as in many commercial composting preparations.

B. Insect Repellents without Chemicals

1. Plant marigolds near vegetables, especially tomatoes, to discourage tomato worms and nematodes.
2. Plant chives near roses to repel aphids.
3. Mint and garden herbs planted near the back door keep flies away.
4. Tansy will discourage ants.
5. Soak onion tops in water for 24 hours. Spray the solution on roses to kill aphids.
6. Don't kill ladybugs. They eat aphids, spiders, and mites.
7. Encourage toads to live in your garden. They eat great quantities of insects.
8. Build a martin or swallow house. These birds eat their own weight in insects in a season. They specialize in mosquitoes.
9. Plant castor beans to discourage moles. (The beans are poisonous, however, so remove them as soon as they form.)
10. Dried lavender, peppermint and pyrethrum hung in closets discourage moths and mice.

21. Recycling Area

Keep an area in your garage, shed or basement where your family can store materials such as glass, cans, newspapers, corrugated cardboard and stationery for recycling. Store the different items in separate containers until the family car is available to deposit the materials at your nearest recycling depot. Perhaps you could encourage reluctant recyclers in your neighbourhood by storing and delivering their items for them. More details on the preparation of materials for recycling are mentioned in the introduction of the book. One of the most valuable areas in your home could be your junk box. This is where you can store all the odds and ends that look as if they have interesting potential. Some rainy day or moment of need you will find there just what you need to fix or make or create something. The personal satisfaction you receive from the money you have saved and the object you have created will be your reward.

v recreation room decorating

1. Joy Logs

A. Richman's Logs
Materials

Old newspapers
Chemicals (see below)
Strong cord
Large container, i.e. plastic garbage pail or cauldron

Method
1. Roll about 20 sheets of newspaper tightly into a log about 12'' or 14'' long
2. Tie securely with strong cord and fasten with a reef knot.
3. Mix the following solution and let logs soak for one week:
   - 2 lbs. coarse salt (a pickling salt)
   - 2 gals. boiling water
   - 1 oz. strontium nitrate
   - 2 lbs. bluestone (for blue flame)
   - 1 oz. bizmuth (for crimson flame)
   - 1 oz. barium or borax (for green flame)
   - (Chemicals may be bought in drug store)
4. Lay paper logs on end in solution and soak about 3 days.
5. Turn, placing other end down, for the last 4 days. Use gloves or wash immediately as chemicals are poisonous.

Cautions:
1. Solution is poisonous.
2. Do not put in a metal container; a plastic garbage pail is fine. If only a metal container is available, line it with a plastic garbage bag that is leakproof.
3. Don't pack the container too tightly with logs as they swell when wet and could split the bucket.
4. Remove and dry for 4 or 5 weeks well out of the reach of children.

5. To decorate logs wrap in some of last year's Christmas paper. They enhance any hearth fire with their colored flames. When making the rounds during Christmas visiting, the logs make the perfect little "made-it-ourselves" gift.

B. Poorman's Logs
Use exactly same method as in A, using a solution made from boiling water and coarse salt only.
These logs burn with a blue flame. Just plain soaking in water, then drying will make logs that will burn at a slower rate than the unsoaked kind.

C. Lazyman's Logs
Materials

>   20" length of 1" dowel or old broom handle
>   Old newspapers

Method
1. Cut a 16" slot down the centre of the dowel or broom handle.
2. Insert a section of newspaper in the slot as shown, then roll it up—snug, but not too tight.
3. When one section of newspaper is half rolled, insert another section with the folded edge on the opposite side.
4. Continue until the log is 2½"-3" in diameter, and then withdraw the rolling tool.
5. Tie the rolled log at each end with soft wire or garbage bag twists. Don't use string. Each log will burn for about 2 hours.

2. Fire Starters

A. Orange Peels
1. Save orange peels and spread them out to dry in a warm place to prevent moulding. These peels act as a kindling and burn with an orange fragrance and blue flame.

B. Candle Ends
1. Save your little bit-ends of candles. When lit and placed under fireplace logs they burn enough to catch the kindling.

3. Wastepaper Baskets

A. Woven Newspaper Basket

Materials

> Newspaper
> Corrugated paper
> Glue
> Kitchen knife
> Paint

Method

1. Open double sheet of newspaper and lay flat on table.
2. Start at bottom and fold up whole sheet until you have a strip about 1″ wide.
3. Glue strip to prevent unravelling. Make 16 strips.
4. Cut 2 circles of corrugated cardboard about 7″ in diameter. Just trace around a pot lid.
5. Glue 9 of the strips to 1 circle of cardboard to resemble spokes of a wheel.
6. Glue the second circle over this to form inside floor of basket.
7. Make 7 rings using newspaper strips and glue them shut. First circle is 7½″ in diameter. All other circles are ½″ larger than one preceding, i.e. 8″, 8½″, 9″, 9½″, 10″, 10½″.
8. Place smallest circle over hub of wheel and begin to weave the spokes up through it.
9. Place second smallest circle on next and do basket weaving (going over one, under next, over next, under etc.) with the straight strips.
10. Press rings firmly down toward base.
11. Continue with all circles finishing with largest.
12. Fold strips over, trim ends and tuck in out of sight behind ring on the inside.
13. Paint to suit your taste. Basket can vary in size depending on number of strips or circles included. Jardinieres can be made by the same method but much narrower strips are used.

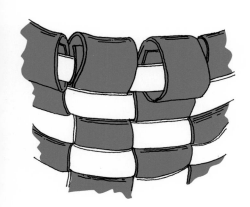

B. Bucket Wastebasket
Materials

Use cardboard buckets such as potato-chip or fried-chicken bucket

Method
1. Decorate bucket by covering with cloth, paper or pictures cut from magazines, i.e. flower pictures from seed catalogue.
2. Varnish, shellac or use a hair spray for protective finish.

C. Styrofoam Basket
Materials

6 styrofoam egg cartons
9″ foil pie-plate
Spread tacks

Method
1. Remove lids of cartons leaving lip edge of bottom half for joining.
2. Fasten bottom sections of 6 crates into circle using spread tacks (about 3 to a section) to fasten flap to edge. The foil pie-plate should fit exactly in bottom for floor of basket.
3. Cut top edge of waste basket to follow contour of carton curves. Variations can be made by reversing the crates so bumps face inside. Basket can be made with 3 cartons using both tops and bottoms. The print on the lid section can be covered with paint specified for use on styrofoam, or with cloth or pictures. The baskets can also be decorated with egg-carton flowers described on page 101. In place of spread tacks, the cartons could be laced together with yarn.

4.   Beaded Curtains or Wall Partitions

1.   See method in Chapter II, page 7 for making paper beads.
2.   Thread beads on nylon stocking cut in spirals and knotted between each bead.
3.   Dye the nylons to match your color scheme. These strings of beads make an effective doorway drape. If your room is wallpapered you could make the beads from leftover scraps and it will tie in very nicely with the decor.

5.   Lampshades

A.   Swag Lampshade
Materials

> 5 cardboard egg cartons
> 60 alleys and glue
> Wire socket support from old lamp
> Stove-pipe wire
> Makes lampshade 1′ tall, diameter 7″

Method

1.   Remove lid section of 5 egg cartons leaving lip edge for joining.
2.   Fasten bottom sections of cartons as explained in method for styrofoam basket, page 62
3.   Press and glue an alley into the middle of each hump.
4.   A coat hanger bent into a circle will help shade retain the circular shape.
5.   Scrounge a wire socket support from an old lamp shade that is destined for the trash heap. Bend it to fit the opening of your shade and fasten in top of the shade using stove-pipe wire. Don't use bulbs stronger than 40 watts. This shade throws a pretty sparkle when light shines through the colored glass.

B. Tiffany Lampshade
Materials

100 plastic or styrofoam cups, 7-oz. size
Bondfast glue for styrofoam
Model glue for plastic
Coat hanger
Pliable wire

Method
1. Glue 22 cups with rims, heels and sides touching to form a circle.
2. Place a second row of cups over the first row with cups resting between cups on first row in bricklaying fashion. The second row will consist of 21 cups.
3. Repeat for 3 more rows, diminishing 1 cup per row.
4. Cut a coat hanger and bend wire to form a circle 6" in diameter. This will fit inside the shade.
5. Wire, socket and bulb will fasten to this wire frame with pliable wire and hold the bulb at a safe distance from the shade.

Hint
A smaller lampshade can be made using this method and the little creamers that come with coffee.

6. Table Lamp

Materials

Wine bottle or jug with reasonably wide base, approximately 6" in diameter
Suggested hardware (socket, cord, sleeve, electric cord, etc.)

Method
1. Choose a jug with an appealing design which will sit firmly and steadily on a table.
2. The bulb and fitting can be purchased in a hardware or electrical supply store, or taken from an old, discarded lamp. Two types of fittings can be used. The first type holds the bulb and fits into the neck of bottle but the cord comes out of the fitting above the bottle line. This is the best type of fitting if you want the bottle base left

clear inside and undecorated. The second fitting is similar in every way except that the cord comes out at the bottom of the fitting. In this case a small hole must be drilled in the bottle with a carbaloide drill.

3. The bottle can be left plain or covered with papier-mâché, stones or shells set in salt-flour-water plaster, or covered with tissue and glue. The bottle can be filled with sand or other interesting materials such as dried coffee grounds, or pumpkin or squash seeds.

7. Umbrella Stand

Materials
4 large juice cans (48-oz. size)
Old fabric or upholstery material

Method
1. Remove the bottoms of 2 cans and the tops of all 4 cans.
2. Fasten cans, open ends together, with masking tape.
3. Make separate slipcovers for each double can.
4. Stitch the 2 slipcovered columns together with a running stitch, making sure there is extra strength at top and bottom edges.
5. Tuck cover in over rim at top and glue to inside of can.
6. Tuck under bottom edges of cover and glue to bottom of cans.
7. Cut cardboard shape exactly the shape of bottom of 2 columns combined and cover with same fabric.
8. Stitch to lower edge of cans.
9. Decorate with sewing notions, such as fringe or braid. If extra weight is needed to balance a heavy umbrella, just put a rock in the bottom of each can.

8. Footstool

Materials

> 7 large juice cans (48 oz.)
> Old fabric
> Corrugated cardboard
> Scraps of fringe, braid, cord, etc. from the sewing
> basket
> Needle
> Thread .
> Kitchen knife

Method

1. Sew a slipcover for each can with fabric made from a cast-off garment or drapery.
2. Position cans, 1 in the centre and 6 around it, as shown in diagram, and sew all edges together top and bottom where they touch.
3. Cut corrugated cardboard with knife to exactly fit shape made by joined cans. Make one section to fit top and another for the bottom.
4. Cover bottom section with same fabric used to cover cans and sew to the covered cans using a slipstitch all around the edge.
5. Pad top section slightly with old nylons, foam rubber or shredded fabric, or even the lint saved from your dryer.
6. Cover top section in the same way as the bottom, and slipstitch to the top of the covered cans.
7. To hide seams, decorate with odds and ends of trim, braid, fringe, rickrack, etc.

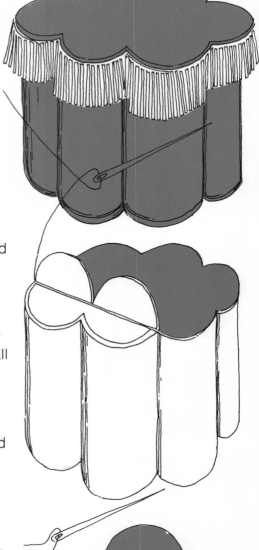

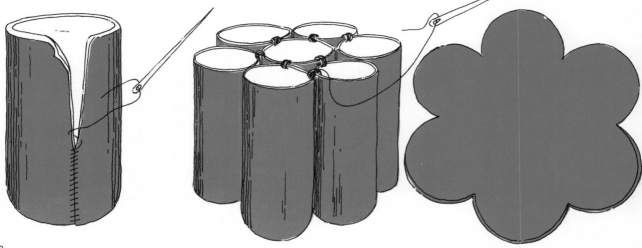

66

9. End Table

Materials

72 pop cans
Corrugated paper
Epoxy glue
Paint

Method

1. Pop cans with shoulders are best for this job as this gives a larger surface area for glue when sides touch. Coke and Fanta orange are examples of such cans. Glue cans together in groups of 4 by spreading glue on the sides of cans. Stand cans in a square, glued sides touching, and hold together with elastic until glue sets.
2. Glue the groups of 4 together.
3. Eventually make 3 blocks of 24 cans and glue the 3 layers together.
4. Be very accurate about keeping the blocks of cans square.
5. Vary the size and height of table by adding or subtracting number of cans.
6. Make top of table from corrugated paper, a piece of window glass, or plywood.
7. Glue top on can base and paint.

Hint

A word to the wise. I naturally assume that those of you who are interested in ecology wouldn't let a pop tin inside your home, and are confirmed "returnable only" pop consumers. However you may have bought tins in a moment of weakness, or perhaps obtained them because you have become a litter cleaner-upper or a garbage picker. When you finally see that mass of 72 cans before you and realize that it only represents 72 drinks, you will have visible proof of the mountains of garbage our society can create. One returnable bottle makes 24 trips before it is discarded. So 3 returnable bottles is equivalent to the 3 cases of pop tins in your table. Use this table as an object lesson to convince your family and friends to press for a ban on non-returnable pop bottles and cans.

10. Coffee Table

Materials
12 sq. ft. of scrap plywood or very heavy corrugated cardboard

Section of plate glass (suggested size 2' x 4')

Method
1. Make 2 - 12" hollow cubes from plywood or a size to suit your taste.
2. Paint.
3. Broken window glass can be cut and bevelled at hardware or glass dealers.
4. Place glass as a bridge over cubes.

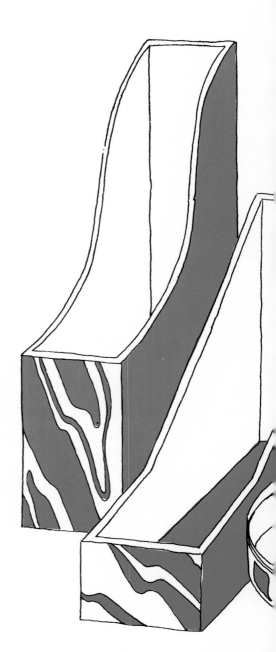

11. Desk File

Materials
Cereal boxes

Scrap paper or material

Cardboard tubes from paper towel or toilet paper or heavier calendar tubes

Method
1. Cut cereal boxes as shown in diagram.
2. Decorate with scraps of wallpaper to match room, or drapery fabric or paint. Several of these can be used together on a desk.
3. Cut wide-based heavy tube about 2" long, and a small tube about 6" long.
4. Cover tubes with same fabric or paint to match boxes.
5. Glue tubes together all sides touching and glue also to styrofoam or corrugated-paper base. The base can also be made large enough to contain the boxes as well as the tubes.
6. Paint the base. The boxes will hold books or correspondence and the tubes will hold pencils, ruler, paper clips, etc.

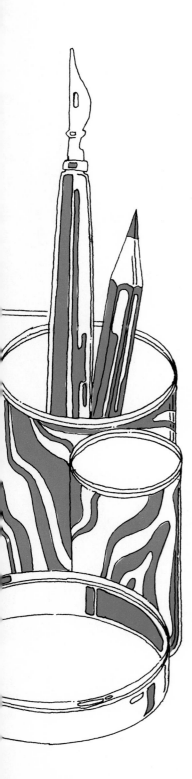

12. Inexpensive, Easy-to-Make Book Shelves

Board and Bottle Shelves
Materials

> 8 wine bottles similar in size and shape
> Scrap lumber or wood from packing boxes

Method
1. Paint pop or wine bottles to match color scheme in room.
2. Paint or stain boards.
3. Cut lengths of board to fit space available for shelves.
4. Straddle boards over the bottles and secure to bottles with Epoxy glue.
5. Use two bottles at each end of each shelf. If you are making a long shelf use 2 more bottles in middle as support. You can also substitute bricks for bottles as the shelf supports.

13. More Hints for Fun Furniture

There are many types of homemade furniture that can be built easily and cheaply e.g. a table can be made from an old slab door and the table legs can be purchased from a hardware or department store and screwed on. Furniture can also be made from logs of rolled newspaper. To make the logs roll newspaper sheets very tightly over a dowel to form logs about 1½″ in diameter. Soak in a weak solution of wallpaper paste. Tie or tape together until dry, making sure they are symmetrical. When they have hardened they can be cut with straight edges and mitred for corner fittings. Build furniture with them as you would with real logs and glue with white or Epoxy glue. Paint.

Don't forget about that old sea trunk you were going to throw away. It can be painted with enamel paint or decoupaged using labels from liquor bottles or pictures of ships, etc. It would make a terrific coffee table and give you storage space as well. A bushel basket painted or stained can also make a unique waste basket.

vi cottage and camping aids

Garbage in cottage country is a real problem. When we get back to nature we become more sensitive to the things that spoil its beauty, and more aware of pollution and litter. Perhaps we also become more aware of packaging excesses when we must personally dispose of our refuse with more effort than just a step toward the garbage can. Summer is also the season we can take time for "do-it-yourself" projects; we are away from society's pressures and do not feel the need to go first-class all the time. A bit of creativity enhances our feelings of worth about ourselves, stretches the holiday dollars and can do wonders to reduce the garbage problem.

For starters, the compost on your cottage property is just as valuable as in the city garden. There is usually an abundance of leaves to cover the peelings etc. if rocky terrain means soil is at a premium. An extra bonus for the fisherman is the wealth of lovely worms that hang out in a compost pit. You can also use bits of meat scraps and fish entrails for bait. Why deplete the lake fish by using minnows, or those valuable insect consumers, the frogs? By the way, friend seagull is the garbage collect of the sky. All sorts of Jonathan Livingstones will be right on deck to help dispose of food scraps and fish entrails. If the fisherfolk in your camp are too squeamish to use the suggested bait, a pair of tin snips and an old can lid can make a personalized lure.

Next step. Burn your paper garbage either by twisting it into rolls to use in the fireplace or camp fire, or make an incinerator from an oil drum. Check for permission and safety rules with the fire ranger.

Never, if avoidable, buy products in plastic containers, as they are nonbiogradable and, as yet, non-recyclable. However if you must, they do make non-breakable containers, and can be cut with scissors to make berry buckets and children's sand toys or lanterns (see pages 12, 7, 47) Get into the habit of using soap or phosphate-free detergent for laundry, dishes and shampoos. Keep those lakes alive and sparkling blue. Hang on to those chunks of styrofoam that seem to surround so many items we buy nowadays. They make excellent fillers for cracks and crannies in a boat like a Sea Flea. Chunks can be stuffed into a large plastic bag and tied into the nose of the boat. The added buoyancy gives extra assurance that it will stay afloat if it flips, and it doesn't add to the weight. A couple of old licence plates, jammed into the sand, and the rack from a stove provides a make-shift hibachi. Actually there isn't much that comes into the cottage that must go out as garbage before it is given another use. Glass jars can be used as refrigerator jars and to store food stuffs away from mice, moths and other insects. Cans can be flattened and recycled. It isn't all that hard to lug them home if there is no depot in the vicinity. As for the other junk that every family accumulates, whatever you do with it, I am sure that you will never resort to becoming a lake-dumper.

1. Boat Bailer

This is the same scoop made from a 48-oz. plastic bottle with side handle and cut with a wide scoop edge, as is described in Chapter II, page 7. Tie the handle to the seat of the boat and you will have it come rain or shine if that proverbial leak gets bigger than your thumb. The scoop along with the bucket and funnel described in Chapter I will provide many hours of sand play for small fry.

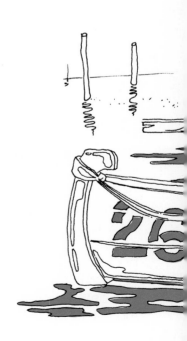

2. Float for Boat or Cottage Keys

1. Cut a piece of styrofoam from a packing carton and put a wire through it and your keys. A cord from a bottle or small block of light wood will serve the same purpose. If you paint the cork or wood with fluorescent paint you will be able to find them in the dark.

3. Boat Bumpers

Materials
    Plastic bottles (32-oz. size, with side handle)
    Nylon cord

Method
1. Tie 3 or 4 plastic bottles through handles on nylon cord making spaces of about 2 feet between each one.
2. Put caps tightly on bottles so they will hold air.
3. If more weight is needed add a little water or sand.
4. Fasten ends of cord to front and back of boat. This bumper string can be lowered over the outside of the boat to prevent scratching and denting of the boat's hull against the dock. A string of bumpers can be made for each side of the boat and fastened independently to inside fitting of boat to be used when needed.

4. Dock Bumpers

1. Cut old tires in sections about 1' long.
2. Spread and nail to side of dock. Now your boat won't be scratched when it bumps up against the dock. An old garden hose can also be used for this purpose.

5. Megaphone

Materials
Large plastic jug (gal. size)

Method
1. Cut cap ring off top of jug and bind with tape to protect mouth.
2. Cut bottom out of jug. Carry in a boat to call for help if trouble arises or to warn other boats in a fog. It is also useful for calling messages ship to shore, or rounding up the gang for dinner.

6. Buoys

Materials
White plastic jugs with handles (48-oz. size)
Nylon rope
Anchors as described on page 75

Method
1. White jugs are best as they are visible even at night. Put lids tightly on jugs so they will hold air and float.
2. String nylon rope through handles and tie so they won't slip. Leave several feet between each jug.
3. Using more nylon cord, fasten string in several places to an anchor to prevent drifting. These buoys can be used to cordon off a suitable swimming area.

Hint
Anchor single jugs over rocks and danger spots as warning signals to boats. The plastic is weatherproof, floats and is soft enough not to damage a boat that might sideswipe it. If white jugs are used they are more easily seen at night as they reflect light.

7. Moorings and Anchors

An old wheel or tire filled with rocks and submerged makes a good mooring for a sailboat. Again, your plastic-jug marker anchored to it will mark the spot on the surface of the water. Another type of mooring or anchor can be made by filling a gallon can or pail with cement and letting it harden. Fasten a rope to the handle of the pail or can. A gallon juice can can also be used. Imbed a piece of heavy chain or make a U bend in an iron rod and let cement form around it. This will make a firm attachment for fastening rope.

8. Marshmallow Toaster or Weiner Roaster

1. Cut hook off a coat hanger, straighten and use as a
    skewer. Wrap the end in a cloth for a heat-proof
    handle. It is wise to carry these skewers on a picnic
    instead of depending on your trusty scout knife to cut
    a switch from a tree. The bark on some trees is
    poisonous, and in winter it is particularly difficult to
    determine one twig from another.

9. Picnic Dishes

A tin can will make a first-rate cooking pot over a
camp fire. Who cares if it gets a black bottom? If you
have brought a good pot and turned it black, rub it
with fine sand and soap to restore the lustre. "Make
your own" plastic dishes are described in the chapter
on Kitchens. Using soft plastic dishes eliminates the
chance of leaving broken bits of glass or hard plastic
chips in picnic areas. As you pack for home look back
to see if you have left any litter, and check that your
campfire is out. Douse with an extra pail of water just
to be on the safe side.

10. Flashlight Guard

Materials
48-oz. juice can or plastic bottle

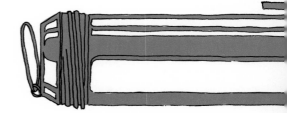

Method
1. Cut hole in bottom of tin can, sized to fit the flashlight.
2. Put neck of flashlight through the hole.
3. Carry by the back of the flashlight. This guard
    intensifies light in one direction. A similar effect can be
    obtained by using a plastic jug, with a handle on top.
    This handle makes it easy to carry the light.

11. Beach Bag

Materials

Old hat or sweater sleeve
Plastic jug (gal. size)
Decorator tape
Knife, ice pick or nail
Yarn and needle
Cord, 1½" long

Method

1. Take a 10" long portion of the old hat or sweater sleeve and sew end turned over 1" to form a casing.
2. String cord through casing for the drawstring.
3. Cut neck and shoulder from plastic jug and keep bottom portion.
4. Punch holes 1" apart around the top edge of the jug with an ice pick or nail.
5. Turn hat or sleeve material inside out and sew the raw edge of the material to the top of the jug stitching through the punctured holes.
6. Pull hat up and right side out.
7. Make a face on the jug by using decorator tape to make eyes, mouth, etc.

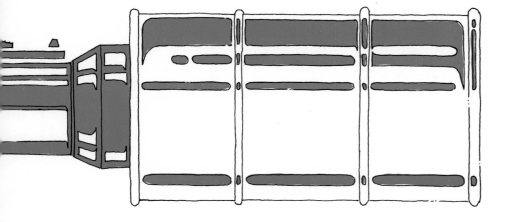

vii christmas and party decorations

1.   Wreaths

A.   Businessman's Wreath
Materials

   Computer cards
   Corrugated cardboard
   Staples
   Paint

Method
1.   Collect about 3 dozen old department store bills or similar computer cards.
2.   Cut corrugated cardboard into 1' square.
3.   Begin by folding one end of cards to form points and staple shut. See method in diagram.
4.   Staple these cards in a circle around corrugated cardboard.
5.   Make a second row inside the first, letting the points fall between the points of the first row.
6.   Continue the same in a third row.
7.   Decorate the centre with an old Christmas corsage, pine cones or bows.
8.   Paint or gild wreath.
9.   Put a loop of string through the cardboard back to hang it.

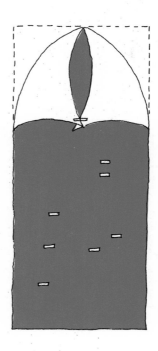

B.   Plastic Bag Wreath
Materials

Metal coat hanger
Plastic bags (if you are using bread bags, you'll need
45-50. Plastic cleaners' bags are also good for this
project)

Method
1.   Spread and bend hanger into a circle.
2.   Cut plastic in strips about 1″ x 6″.
3.   Tie the strips around the hanger and pack tightly
together.
4.   Fluff out plastic and trim unwanted ends.
5.   Either trim to make very symmetrical or leave uneven
to suit your taste.
6.   Decorate if desired with paint or gilt.
7.   Pin on a colored bow or Christmas ornament.

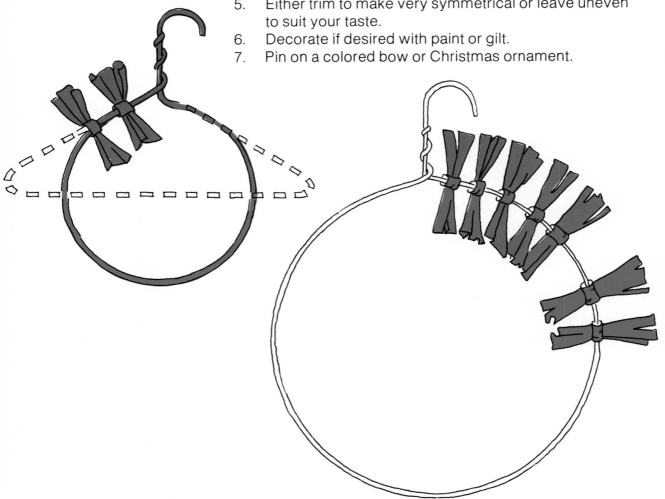

2. Magazine Paper Sculpture

A. Christmas Tree
Materials

Old Reader's Digest or a similar size of magazine with cover removed
Paint

Method
1. Fold page of magazine as shown. Crease the first two folds firmly.
2. Roll remaining pages right into centre of the book and do *not* crease.
3. Keep following this method on all the pages until every page of the book is used up. It will hold its own shape.
4. Paint with gilt.
5. Put a paper star on top with a bit of wire or toothpick.

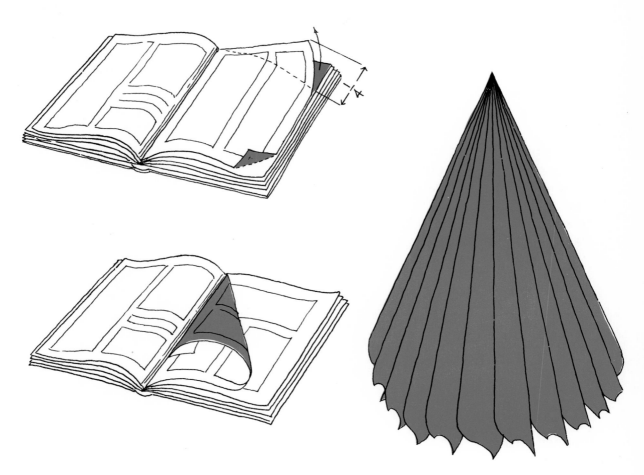

B.   Paper Angel
Materials

> Small magazine such as Reader's Digest with cover removed
> Styrofoam ball
> Paint

Method
1.   Use the same method as in Christmas Tree to form the angel's body.
2.   Replace star with a styrofoam ball as head.
3.   Make hair from string or wool, eyes and mouth from sequins or buttons.
4.   Wings can be made of paper and fastened at the back.
5.   Spraypaint or paint with brush.

C.   Paper Candle
Materials

> Small magazine, i.e. Reader's Digest, with cover removed
> Toothpick
> Paint

Method
1.   Use same method of folding magazine as in Christmas Tree except that only one perpendicular fold is made in centre of page and page is rolled toward centre from that fold.
2.   Use a toothpick for wick.
3.   Paint.

3.   Candles

Materials
> 1-qt. cardboard milk carton or plastic ice-cream carton
> Old candle stubs
> Paraffin saved from jam jars
> Crushed ice
> Butcher cord
> Crayons

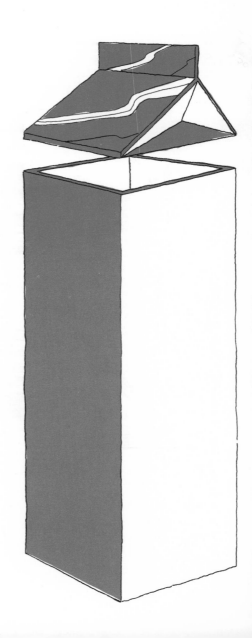

Method

1. Clean milk carton and cut off top just at point where carton slopes inward.
2. Oil inside of carton with vegetable oil.
3. Fasten cord to centre bottom and tie centre top on a pencil which is straddling the carton.
4. Fill carton with coarsely crushed ice.
5. Pour over the ice a mixture of melted wax which has been colored by adding melted broken crayons or colored candle stubs. Remember color chart when combining colors, i.e. yellow and blue make green.
6. When wax hardens pour off water and tear off carton.
7. Remove pencil and trim cord wick.

Caution

Be very careful when melting the wax as it is highly inflammable. Always use low heat and never leave it unattended.

4. Festive Candleholders

A. Plastic
Materials

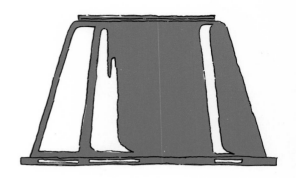

> 5 plastic containers of the type used for yoghurt,
>   cottage cheese, head cheese, etc.
> White glue
> Sewing odds and ends
> Paint
> Shellac

Method

1. Glue containers together with white glue to form a shape that turns you on.
2. Cover from top to bottom with narrow strips of newspaper which have been dipped in a solution of water and wallpaper paste.
3. Shape and mould the papier-mâché with your hands until smooth. Let dry overnight.
4. Glue on decorations of buttons, lace, rickrack, string, etc.
5. Paint. Dark paint can be rubbed over top and into curves if an antique effect is desired.
6. Shellac or varnish.

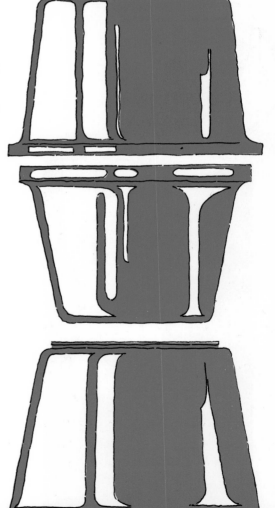

B.   Glass Jars
Materials

A collection of assorted glass jars
Epoxy glue
Corrugated cardboard
Paint

Method
1.   Cut circles of corrugated cardboard slightly larger than base of jars.
2.   Glue jars and cardboard in layers with white glue. Epoxy glue will hold the jars together if you do not want to bother with cardboard rings.
3.   Use the same technique as in A to cover with strips of paper dipped in wallpaper paste to make papier-mache.
4.   Paint and decorate.

Hint

Using the same method as in A and B, candleholders can also be made from assorted tin cans. i.e. 2 10-oz. soup cans and 2 6-oz. tuna cans. These make fun candleholders for your holiday candles or they could hold climbing plants such as ivy.

5. Christmas Door Ornaments

A. Bells
Materials

Tin can lids and bottoms of various sizes—2 or 3 of
 each of 48-oz., 14-oz. and 10-oz. cans
Tin snips
Thin-nosed pliers
Thick yarn, old nylon stocking or cranberries strung on
 strong thread

Method
1. Use snips to cut can lids into 4 sections as shown in
 diagram.
2. Punch hole in centre of lid using a hammer and nail.
3. Use pliers to bend the sections forward until they
 meet.
4. Thread the bells on yarn or nylons cut into spiral strips
 or on cranberry ropes.
5. Hang at random heights and gather into a cluster
 fastened with a bow. As the door opens or closes the
 bells will greet visitors with a merry tinkle.

B. Christmas-Tree Door Hanging
Materials

Cardboard, 2' x 1'
Wood shavings
Paint
White glue

Method
1. Cut cardboard in shape of Christmas tree.
2. Spread generously with glue.
3. Press wood shavings or other suitable media such as
 milkweed pods, paper curls or excelsior onto the glue
 until background is covered.
4. Leave in its natural state or paint.
5. Tape a loop of cord to the back of the tree for
 hanging.
6. Tree can be decorated with acorns or walnut halves
 and ribbons.

6. Angels

Materials

Cardboard about the weight of the type used to make
    a suit box (a large coat box lid would make an angel
    about 14″ high)
Old cotton sheet or pillowcase
Styrofoam ball
String trimmings
Wallpaper paste
Coat hanger
Paint, staples, tape
Doily or lace
Pliers

Method

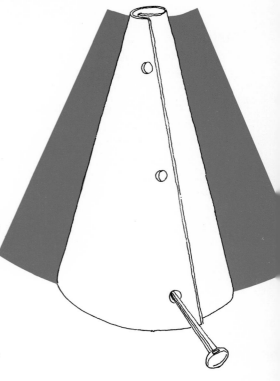

1. Form a cone from cardboard. The height of cone will determine height of angel.
2. Either staple or use spread tacks to hold the cone shape.
3. Tear old sheet or pillowcase in strips, first piece 6″ wide and 1′ long.
4. Second piece should be about 16″ wide and length about 8″ plus twice the height of the cone. (If your cone is 10″ then cloth strip should be 28″ long.)
5. Cut hook off a coat hanger and bend to form shoulders, arms, a point to hold head and one to fit into top of cone. You will need pliers and a strong grip to bend a coat hanger. If you lack the muscles necessary, use a piece of finer wire. See diagram.
6. Fit wire into top of cone and tape to make secure.
7. Make a mixture of wallpaper paste and water using about 1 cup paste to 1 qt. water. Paste should be consistency of pea soup.
8. Work with angel form on a tray or something portable, because you won't be able to pick up the angel till it dries.
9. Dip the small piece of sheeting into the paste and squeeze out so it won't be drippy. Drape the wet sheeting over the shoulders and down arms, forming a wide sleeve.
10. Cut a small hole in centre of large piece of sheeting.
11. Dip this piece into solution. Squeeze out most of the paste but leave it quite wet.

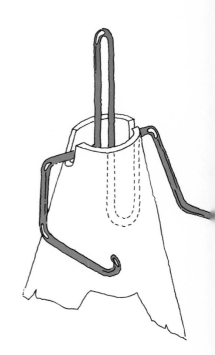

12. Fit wire for head through the hole and drape sheeting over the cone.
13. Now arrange the front section in folds for the skirt.
14. Drape the back section of sheeting and bring it around to overlap front section, and the sleeve pieces.
15. Fold under the raw edges.
16. If a sash is desired braid string and dip in paste and fit it under the back drape and over the front.
17. Dip little pieces of tissue in paste and wad it over the wire for hands.
18. If you want your angel to hold a little candle or book put it into the hands. A straight pin could be useful to hold the object in place.
19. Fit a doily over head wire and put across shoulders to make a collar.

20. Slightly carve sides of a styrofoam ball, 2″ in diameter, to make cheeks. Press it onto the head wire.
21. Cut cord into 5″ lengths, dip into paste and lay over ball for hair. Hair can also be made from curls of paper, or yarn.
22. Make hat or halo from small doily or drape head with more cloth dipped in paste.
23. Pin sequins on for eyes and make lashes with curls of paper, and paste these on with white glue.
24. Set the tray holding the figure carefully away, preferably in a warm dry place. It takes from 1 to 2 days to dry thoroughly.
25. Decorate with a paint especially marked as suitable for paper and styrofoam. Use your imagination and vary this figure to make choir boys, wise men, or an entire nativity scene.

7. Tin Christmas Tree

Materials

    Tin can tops and bottoms—3 each of 48-oz., 19-oz., 10-oz. and 6-oz. sized cans
    Tin snips
    Wire coat hanger
    Flat 2-oz. can
    Epoxy glue

Method

1. Mark lids and bottoms in quarters with a pen or pencil.
2. Make a small hole in the centre of lids by hammering a nail through it.
3. Starting mid-point in one of the quarter sections of a lid, cut a curved slit toward the centre, stopping about ¼" from centre of lid. Continue to cut slits ⅛" wide until half of the quarter section is cut into slits. Turn the lid over and repeat the same method until another half of a quarter section is cut. The slits will curl in opposite directions. Continue to cut slits using this method until the circle is completed. Cut all the lids using this method.
4. Cut a section from a wire coat hanger about 12" long and straighten it.
5. Push the hanger through the puncture in each cut lid starting with the largest lid and graduating to the smallest. Space each section evenly to form the tree shape.
6. Puncture the bottom of the 2-oz. flat tin in the same way as was done to the lids.
7. Push the hanger with attached lids into the hole in the flat tin which will now be the base for the tree.
8. Cut two small stars from tin-can lids and fasten them back-to-back over the protruding wire at the top of the tree. You could also top the tree off with a small tree ornament.

Hint:

The same method can be used to make a Christmas tree from styrofoam meat trays. Use scissors instead of tin snips and a chunk of styrofoam for the tree base. When the styrofoam discs are placed on the wire hanger, it will be necessary to place 4 or 5 small styrofoam discs between the branches as spacers on the hanger.

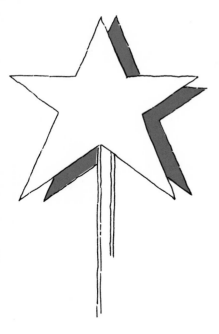

8. Tree Ornaments

A. Styrofoam
Materials

> Pieces of styrofoam from packaging
> Pins
> Sequins
> Buttons
> Old earrings and broken jewellery
> Wool
> Braid

Method
1. Cut the styrofoam in balls, squares, triangles, etc.
2. Wrap with wool or tin foil or leave bare.
3. Glue or pin on sequins and other decorations.
4. Pin a loop of ribbon on top to fasten to Christmas tree.

B. Meat Tray Discs
Materials

> Felt scraps
> Styrofoam meat trays
> Coat hanger, thread

Method
1. Make Santa faces on discs cut from meat tray, with scraps of felt. These can make tree ornaments or can be hung by thread as a mobile, from a coat hanger.

C. Tin Christmas-Tree Ornaments
Materials

> Tin can lids and bottoms
> Tin snips
> Small-nosed pliers

Method
1. Cut the tin lids and bottoms with tin snips, starting at the outside edge and stopping about ½" from the centre. Continue to cut in slivers about ⅛" apart. The metal will curl of its own accord.

Variations

1. To make a cup design, use method outlined except cut the slits ¼″ wide. With pliers bend tips in to form points and bend each sliver forward to form cup.
2. To make a snowflake use method outlined and turn each sliver a half turn to the right with pliers.
3. To make a flower use method outlined and use pliers to curl every second sliver toward centre, turning the tip under.
4. To make an angel cut angel shape as in diagram. With pliers, turn skirt section in slight turns, to give a round shape. Make short fringe-like slivers in wing section. Bend wings back and head forward.
5. To make a bell, cut out small triangular sections as shown in diagram on page 90. Bend remaining sections forward to touch each other. Punch a hole in centre with nail and hammer, so thread can be inserted for hanging.

D. Jewellery Ornaments
Materials

Odd earrings, broken bracelets, necklaces, etc.

Method

These odd pieces can be strung together or sewn on felt in loops or 4″ strips to make tree hangings. The tree lights reflect in the glass jewellery, and add sparkle to your tree.

Hint

Tree ornaments can also be made from thread spools painted or wound with cord and decorated with beads or buttons. The plastic "egg" containers for nylons (gross over-packaging) decorate well and make grand and spectacular ornaments. If they are used in halves they resemble bells. Don't forget how suitable these containers could be for making Easter decorations.

9. Santa Jars

Materials
Baby-food jars
Felt scraps

Method
1. Make eyes, beard, moustache and nose from scraps of felt and glue on jars.
2. Sew a little cap to fit over the lid. This jar filled with candy makes a cute gift for a child or favors for a party table.

Hint
Vary this theme and make chicks and bunnies for Easter and cats or witches for Halloween!

10. Table Favors

A. Wheel Barrows
Materials
Egg carton
Plastic straw
Lifesavers

Method
1. Carton humps can be cut as you did for sleigh.
2. Press a plastic straw through the wheelbarrow body as shown.
3. Insert a lifesaver for a wheel, then return the straw through the other side of wheel barrow.

B. Santa's Sleigh
Materials
Styrofoam egg carton
Scissors
Pipe cleaners

Method
1. Cut one hump of carton in a shape that resembles a sleigh.

2.	Use pipe cleaners curled at front, small candycanes or licorice whip pieces for runners.
3.	A drop of white glue will hold on the pipe cleaners. Molasses will hold on candy runners.
4.	Fill with little candies.
5.	Child's name can be put on side of sleigh with a magic marker.

Gift Wraps

It has always seemed ridiculous to me to spend a lot of money for wrapping paper knowing that it will only be discarded. It's more sensible and lots of fun to use your imagination and create packaging that costs you nary a penny. You can use the money saved on the contents of the gift.

To begin, first try to calm the frenzied gift openers so that the used paper can be salvaged—a little trimming of frayed edges and a warm iron can make used paper look like new. Scraps of wallpaper can make delightful wrappings and nylon stockings cut in 1" spiral strips make good ribbon substitutes—they can be dyed exotic colors and are tough enough to use on any type of packaging. Why not make a cluster of styrofoam flowers or a small corsage of fresh or dried flowers from the garden to decorate a package instead of manufactured bows? Or use the comic section from the Sunday newspaper to wrap children's gifts. Your gift wrap can also be just as useful as the gift inside—a "kitcheny" present could be wrapped in a tea towel and decorated with a pot scraper or a bunch of measuring spoons. A little girl's gift can be presented inside the bag described on page 77 or tied with thick yarn she can use later for her ponytail. The bucket described on page 12 could be used to parcel a collection of small gifts with the outside of the bucket decorated to give a hint of the contents. i.e. sports pictures on a bucket containing fishing tackle or glamor shots on a bucket containing perfume or makeup. Perhaps your ingenuity will be catching and the receivers of your gifts will also be converted to new, inexpensive packaging through the use of "throwaways."

viii the old and the new

1. Decoupage Antique Plaque

Materials
Picture suitable for antiquing, taken from Christmas
    card, calendar or magazine
Scrap wood or press board, ¾" thick
Paint
Varnish, shellac or lacquer used in decoupage
Round file
Saw
Fine sandpaper

Method
1. Cut piece of wood slightly larger than the picture you
   are going to use. Make it irregular in shape.
2. With the curved side of a file, bevel and gouge edges,
   round corners and in general give it a worn look.
3. Sand wood until it is smooth.
4. Coat wood with varnish.
5. Make edges of picture irregular or possibly even burn
   or tear edges and crumple.
6. Glue onto plaque with white glue, and smooth out
   from centre to edges. If an air bubble is trapped, prick
   with pin and flatten.
7. Professional lacquers such as Podgy can be
   purchased for this craft and they can be used to stick
   the picture onto wood at this stage.
8. Put a coat of varnish or one of the other products right
   over wood and picture, going over the sides of the
   block. Let dry.
9. Sand lightly or rub with fine steel wool.
10. Use a dark oil-based paint—black, brown, green, blue,
    red—and paint over wood and picture completely.
11. While paint is still wet, take soft gauze or paper tissue
    and starting in middle of the picture rub off just as
    much paint as will give the desired antique effect.
    Some will prefer the picture so dark that it is barely
    visible, while others will want it lighter and only slightly

colored. Always leave the picture darkest at the edges.

12. When the paint has dried lacquer completely, and then sand lightly.
13. Lacquer and sand several times depending upon the state of perfection and the height of gloss you want.

2. Picture Hook

Materials
Zip top from pop tin

Method
1. Flatten zip top.
2. Nail or tack on back of plaque or wall hanging, with loop end up. Loop will bend out enough to hang over a tack on wall. This type of hook is excellent if you want the picture to hang flat against the wall.

3. Decorator Bottles

Jars and bottles can be painted or covered with a variety of materials. Methods simple enough for toddlers or sophisticated enough for artists can be adjusted to match the talents of the individual.

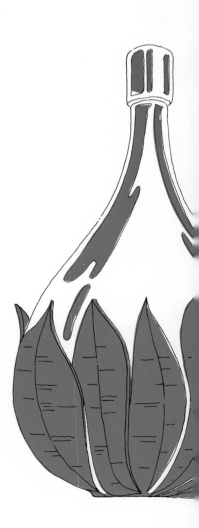

A. Tissue Paper Cover
Tear small irregular pieces of different colored tissue paper and stick on bottle with a thin layer of glue. This gives a stained glass effect.

B. Papier-Mâché Cover
Narrow strips of newspaper dipped in thin wallpaper paste can be layered on a bottle to completely change its shape and design. One method is described in Chapter chapter II, page 31.

C. Yarn or Rope Cover
Yarn or rope can be tightly wound around the surface of a bottle or jar. If there is a definite indentation or curve on the container it helps to put a thin layer of glue in that area before winding material over it. This can be

left in its natural state or painted, varnished or sprayed with hair spray as a protective coating.

D. Shells, Glass Chip Cover
Shells or broken chips of colored glass can be glued directly on a jar or bottle with Epoxy glue or imbedded in a layer of clay, or a salt-flour-water mixture which has been pressed on the surface.

E. Decoupage
Pictures from magazines or cut-outs can be put on surface with the decoupage method.

4. Styrofoam Flowers

Materials
Styrofoam egg cartons
Florist's wire or any flexible wire

A. Roses
1. Cut out 4 humps from a styrofoam egg carton.
2. Cut each hump in 4 or 5 petals as shown.
3. Take first set and scrunch it in to form a bud.
4. Wrap base with Scotch tape to hold in shape.
5. The second is taped the same way only more loosely so that it will fit over the first bud.
6. The last two sections are left as is.
7. Cut a 6″ length of pliable wire and form a small hook on the end.
8. Stick the wire through each section starting with the first cup or bud. The hook will hold so that it won't slide right through.
9. As sections are put on, alternate the petals to make a balanced flower and then pull tightly.
10. A little tape around the wire under rose will hold petals in place.

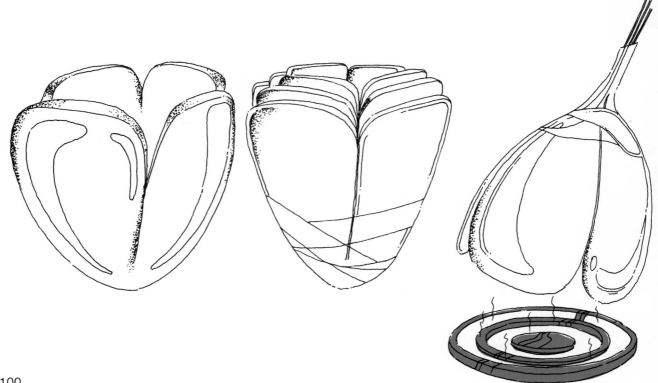

B. Tulips

1. Use the same method and shape as in A but use only 3 humps from egg carton.
2. When completed invert and lower slowly and cautiously down toward a hot stove element or candle flame. This will cause the edges to blunt and curl slightly. As soon as this blunting begins to happen draw instantly away.
3. Wire flowers as shown in A.

C. Mums

1. Use 4 or 5 humps from styrofoam egg carton and the same method as in A and B.
2. Instead of rounding the petals sliver or fringe them as shown.
3. When all sections are assembled rotate cautiously over a hot stove element as explained in B. To make outer petals curl out hold the flower over heat on its side. To make centre petals curl in, invert flower directly over heat. Experiment for different effects.

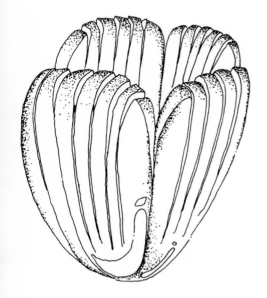

D. Water Lilies

1. Cut wide petals about 2″ long and 1″ wide in a similar way as flowers in A and B, but use styrofoam meat trays instead of egg cartons.
2. To make stamens bundle slivers of styrofoam tightly with thread and curl by using heat as in B and C.
3. Cut lily pads about 6″ in diameter from larger styrofoam meat trays.
4. They can be wired, or glued together with white glue.

Hint

Clusters of these flowers make good substitutes for bows on gift wraps. Nylon stockings cut in spirals to prevent running and dyed, make good strong ribbon substitutes.

E. Plaque

1. Fasten flowers into a gay corsage and mount on styrofoam meat tray.
2. Add trim etc., from sewing basket and you will have a floral spray plaque.

F. Table Centrepiece

1. Fasten flowers closely in a mass to form a design and intersperse with sprigs of evergreen, real, or artificial foliage, to make a flower arrangement for your table.

G. Hanging

1. Make a chickenwire ball and pack it solidly with styrofoam flowers described in A, B and C. The wire stems can be fastened into the chickenwire.
2. Either hang by a cord or put on a stick and place in a flowerpot.

5. Mobiles

A. Styrofoam
Materials

> Styrofoam meat trays
> Coat hanger
> Thread

Method

1. Cut shapes of boats, fish, funny faces, etc., from the meat trays with scissors.
2. Decorate with Magic Markers or cut out felt or cloth pieces and glue to the discs with white glue. The light weight of the styrofoam is an advantage when making a mobile.
3. With wire cutters, remove hook from hanger and straighten. Cut in pieces about 1' long and paint a bright color.
4. Thread discs and string on these wire arms of mobile.
5. Check balance when wires and discs are hung one above the other with thread. Chunks of styrofoam from packing cases can also be carved into shapes and hung as a mobile.

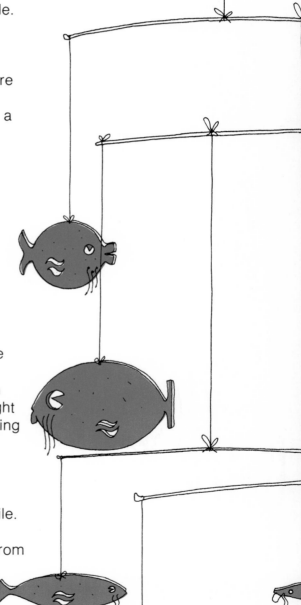

B. Can Lids

1. Crimp the edges of can lids with pincers and paint them.
2. Crush broken glass by putting between sheets of newspaper and hitting with a hammer.
3. Spread glue on can lids and sprinkle with the crushed glass.
4. Hang as described in A.

C. Papier-Mâché

1. Make balls or shaped objects with shredded newspaper soaked in thin wallpaper paste.
2. Insert a loop into ball before it dries.
3. Paint on design and varnish
4. Hang as in A.

6. Terrarium Gardening Tools

A. **Scoop**—Plastic spoon of swizzle stick taped to long stick.

B. **Placer**—Cut and straighten a coat hanger and make a hook on one end. Use this to grasp plants and lower into bottle for planting. The placer can also be used to remove things from the bottle.

C. **Root Loop**—A length of copper wire bent in spiral.

D. **Tamp**—A wooden spool or cork on a long stick makes a useful tamp for pressing soil around roots.

E. **Sponge**—A piece of sponge stuck on straightened hanger can be dampened for wiping the interior of the bottle.

F. **Tweezers**—Split a long piece of bamboo and make a wedge. Use this to grasp things in the bottle.

G. **Cleaner**—A small paint brush taped to a stick can be used to clean the leaves of plants in the terrarium.

H. **Brush**—A bottle brush taped to a stick can be used to swab the sides of the bottle.

I. **Water Bulb**—A kitchen baster can be used to water plants. This will eliminate the splashing of muddy water that might occur if water was poured from a height.

J. **Long-Necked Funnel**—Tape piece of tubing to the cut-off neck of a plastic bottle.

K. **Pruner**—A razor blade taped to a long narrow stick makes a good instrument for removing and cutting leaves, etc.

L. **Hook**—A paperclip bent into a hook and taped to a long stick helps remove debris from the bottom of the terrarium.

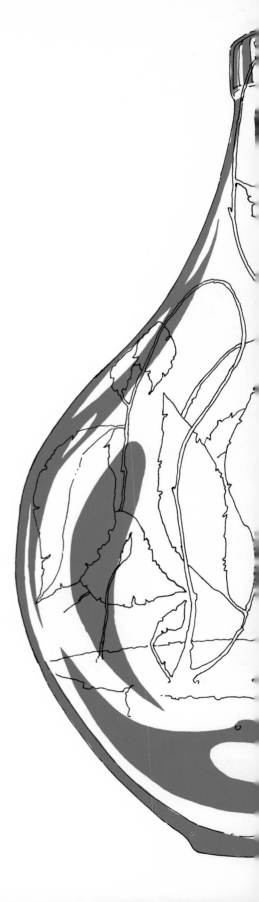

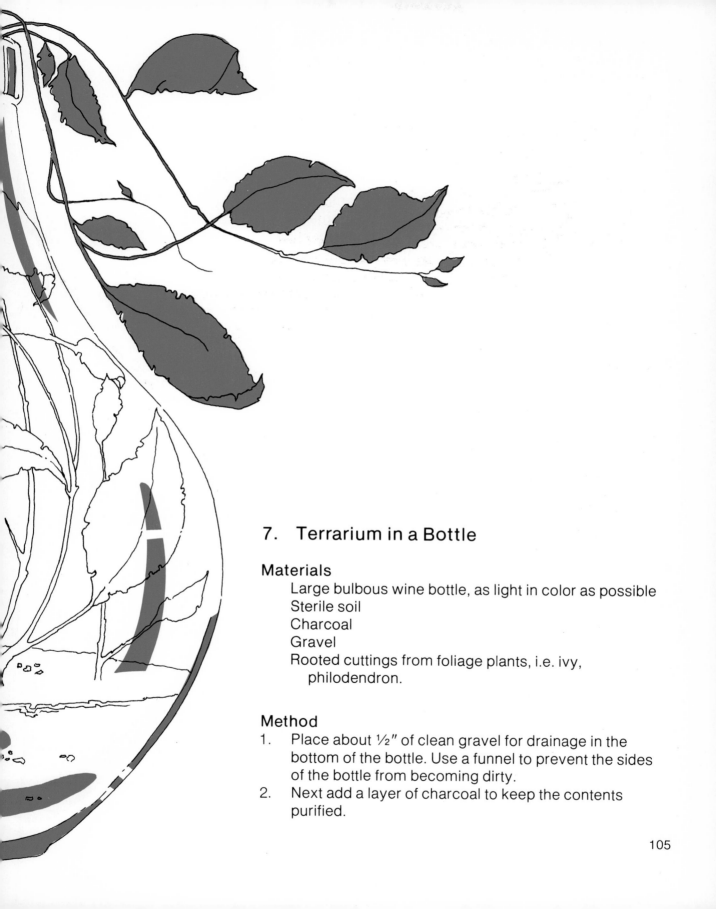

7. Terrarium in a Bottle

Materials
Large bulbous wine bottle, as light in color as possible
Sterile soil
Charcoal
Gravel
Rooted cuttings from foliage plants, i.e. ivy,
    philodendron.

Method
1. Place about ½″ of clean gravel for drainage in the bottom of the bottle. Use a funnel to prevent the sides of the bottle from becoming dirty.
2. Next add a layer of charcoal to keep the contents purified.

3. Next add about 2″ of sterile soil. Either purchase the soil or make your own by baking garden soil at about 400° for 20 minutes. This will kill weed seeds and bacteria.

4. Make sure your rooted cuttings are of a type that won't grow too big for the container. Plant cuttings, using the tools described in 6. Dig small holes where you want your plants positioned. Lower cuttings with the hook and stand them upright.

5. Cover roots with soil using the scoop and tamp. Clean the sides of the terrarium with the sponge or brush.

6. To prevent splashes, water with a kitchen baster or by sucking water up a straw, holding finger over it and directing water to the plant roots. Use only about ⅛ cup of water. Overwatering will cause the terrarium to fog up.

7. Keep plants pruned so they will not grow too large for the terrarium and always cut off dead or sick leaves.

8. Water only if the plants begin to droop and *never* water if condensation forms in the bottle. You may find that the terrarium never needs water again as it creates its own moisture. The water recycles from roots to leaves to roots again in the natural process. This is possible because there is so little evaporation in a small-mouthed bottle. Keep the terrarium in light but not in direct sunshine. Rotate it ¼ of a turn toward the light, twice a week, so that the plants won't grow lopsided.

8. Aquarium in a Bottle

Materials

Large wine bottle or other large glass jug, preferably colorless

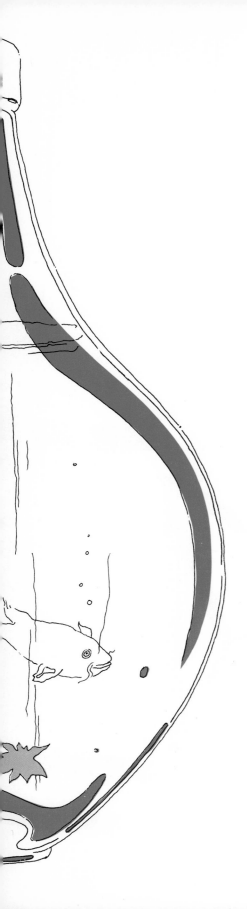

Method
1. If jug has small neck and fish are large it will be necessary to cut a hole large enough with a glass cutter to put hand in. If small fish such as guppies or neons are used, it is possible to operate through the neck.
2. Use a funnel to put about 2″ of sand in bottle.
3. Use tools and methods to plant aquarium plants similar to those used in 6 and 7 for terrarium.
4. Fill with water to within 2″ or 3″ of the top.
5. Put anti-chlorine chemical in water or let water stand a day or two to let chlorine dissipate.
6. Make sure the water in the aquarium is the same temperature as the water where fish are situated before moving them.
7. Keep only 6 small fish in a gallon jug as you will not be able to properly maintain aeration with more.
8. Any dead fish can be removed by drawing them out using the water bulb described on page 104.
9. Keep near light but never in direct sunlight. A small aquarium like this will be more subject to quick temperature changes which is hard on the fish so give this consideration when locating it.

9. Hooked Rug

Cut strips from old, clean garments. Suitable materials are wool, crimplene, nylon stockings. Don't mix types of fabrics in any one rug as they wear or launder differently. Strips should be about ¼" to ½" wide.

A. Base

Base for rug is burlap. This can either be bought in fabric store or made from old potato sacks which have been thoroughly washed. Choose base the size desired for rug plus a 1" border. Design the pattern and draw it on the burlap with a waterproof Magic Marker.

B. Frame

The frame can be made from old wood or sides of a packing case. Build frame as shown in diagram. Top rail and bottom rail are unattached to roll the burlap on while rug is being hooked. These two pieces A and B can be held securely, as rug is worked, by means of C clamps at each of the four corners. For small hooking projects such as cushions, pictures or handbags, frames small enough to hold on your lap should be used. An embroidery hoop or old tennis racquet frame would do as a frame.

TO

E→

BOTTO

F→

NOTE
"C" clamps at E, F, G and H permit rolling of the top and bottom rails. All rails have ⅛ inch holles at 1" intervals to lace in the rug. Use 1" common nails on the end rails.

Strong shelf brackets at A, B, C and D.
Small brackets at E, F, G and H

B

A

Make two rails as shown, to fit
onto the end rails – top one
at E and G – bottom one at F and H.
Shape a half lap joint
at each of these junctions
of the horizontal and end rails
Secure these rails with "C"
clamps.

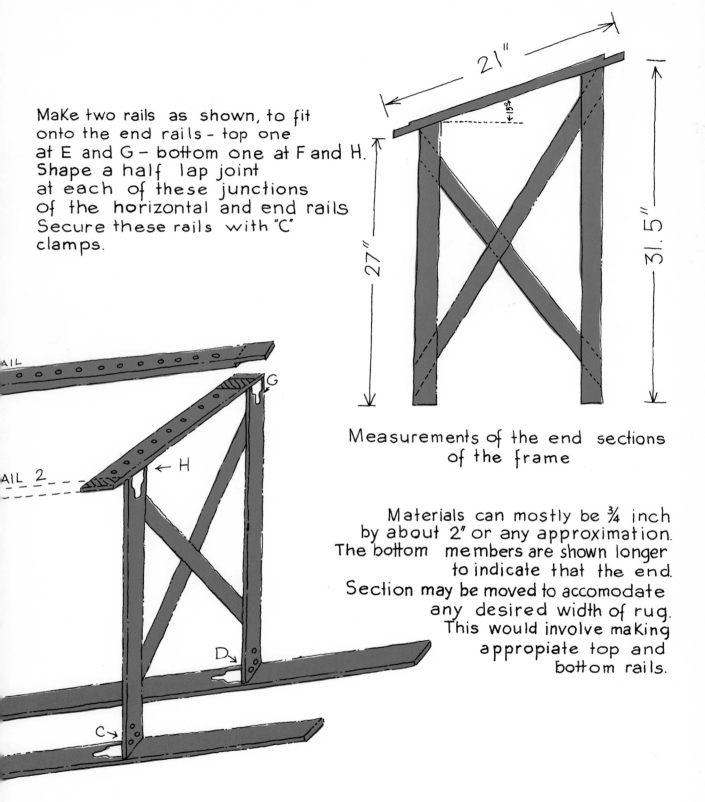

21"

15°

27"

31.5"

Measurements of the end sections
of the frame

Materials can mostly be ¾ inch
by about 2" or any approximation.
The bottom members are shown longer
to indicate that the end.
Section may be moved to accomodate
any desired width of rug.
This would involve making
appropiate top and
bottom rails.

G

AIL

AIL 2

← H

D

C →

C. Rug Hook

Hook can be made with a block of wood or cork as a handle. A spike nail inserted in the handle can be filed at the tip to form hook. See diagram. Hook could also be made by removing all tines but one from an old fork and hooking the tip of the remaining tine.

D. The Rug

To hook the rug, take strip of fabric and hold with left hand on the underside of burlap. Holding hook in right hand poke it through the burlap and raw up a small loop of the fabric. Continue hooking in about every second or third thread of burlap until strip is done or pattern requires another piece. Draw last piece of strip through to top and snip off excess. Always finish on top. Work in random sections and not in even rows. When rug is done remove it from the frame and turn back and glue down the edges. A non-skid paint can be put on reverse side. It helps secure the rug against unravelling.

10. Afghan

Materials
Old socks or sweaters

Method
1. Cut squares from cuffs of old socks or sections of old sweaters that are not too worn.
2. Crochet them together and then crochet a border around the afghan. This makes a warm "throw" for the car or camping.

11. Braided Rug

1. Suitable materials are wool, cotton, crimplene, terry towelling, nylon stockings and plastics. Do not mix types of fabrics in any one rug. Use materials cut from old but clean garments or in case of plastics use bread bags, etc.
2. Cut materials in strips about 2″ wide cutting the ends on a 45° angle. The angle cut means there is less bulkiness when they are joined.
3. Fasten 3 pieces together and braid, turning in raw edges as it progresses.
4. As one strip ends join the next strip with a running stitch. Join as you go and not in advance. Colors can be mixed in all 3 strands of braid or you can keep to a solid color.
5. When several feet of braid are done, stitch loosely in a coil with a strong thread, easing it around the curves. The rug will curl if stitching is too tight.
6. Continue this process until rug is finished. The rugs can be round or oval or long ovals depending on how it is coiled.

Hint
Old bread bags or cleaner's bags, can be crocheted into mats. These plastic mats are handy inside doorways for wet boots.

12. Quilting Frame

Materials
22 feet of 1″ x 2″ board
4 C clamps
Tacks

Method
1. Cut the board into two 5′ and two 6′ lengths.
2. Make a 5′ by 6′ frame by fastening at corners with the C clamps.
3. Prop the frame at the 4 corners on the back of 4 straight-backed chairs.
4. Tack the quilt to the frame or wap material over the frame and sew the quilt to it.

Hint

This makes a suitable quilting frame for a standard 5'
by 6' quilt. Why not cut your quilting pieces from
sewing scraps and old garments? Our grandmothers
did and they were the champion quilters of all time.
Just make sure that you do not combine new materials
with old, as they will likely have a different rate of
wear. You should also be careful about combining
different types of fabrics as they will wash differently
and wear unevenly. The libraries carry a large
selection of craft books which offer many pattern
selections. You could, of course, invent your own
design and make your very own heirloom to pass on
to a new generation.

13. Homespun Yarn

If you own a Samoyed or any other dog that sheds
you can be the potential owner of a beautiful knit
outfit. Save your dog's combings, not the clippings, as
the hair must be shed to be complete. You can have it
carded and spun into beautiful soft yarn. You can do
this yourself if you have access to carders or a
spinning wheel. Simple spinning can be done on a
drop or hand spindle by placing a stick or pencil in a
rubber ball or through a Tinker Toy disc and twirling it
in a small bowl, spinning the yarn as it twirls.

14. Jewellery

A.   Bracelet
Materials

> Large cardboard tube such as the kind used to mail
>   calendars
> Papier-mâché
> Paint
> Odds and ends, i.e. string, buttons

Method
1.   Cut rings from large cardboard tube.
2.   Wrap with papier-mâché made from narrow strips of
     torn newspaper dipped in thin wallpaper paste.

3. Decorate with string, buttons, etc.
4. If no cardboard tube is available a circle can be made by wrapping papier-mâché around a glass jar of the right size. After it has hardened the jar can be pulled out or broken away by wrapping it in a cloth and hitting with a hammer. Paint and lacquer bracelet for protection.

Hint

Earrings, buttons and beads can be made with papier-mache in the same way as the bracelet, but model the shapes freeform. Toothpicks can be inserted to hold spaces for thread holes in the buttons. Ear clasps can be purchased and attached to finished earrings with glue. Fun jewellery can be made by stringing seeds like apple, pumpkin and squash. Try stringing bones, i.e. chicken neck vertebrae which have been boiled, and bleached with laundry bleach, for a unique bracelet.

15. Junk Box Collage and Sculpture

Keep a box of odds and ends of sewing notions, plastics, styrofoam pieces, broken machine parts, wire, furs and fabrics, nuts and bolts, etc. Beautiful wall plaques can be made by blending pieces and parts into a design and mounting them on a background with glue, or by imbedding them in clay or similar media. They can be left in their natural colors or painted a monocolor. Similarly, sculptures can be built with tin cans or any other items from your junk box. A formal sculpture can be designed by drafting out plans for a specific form and building to conform to the design or you may prefer to do a random *objet d'art.* At any rate garbage can be beautiful!

garbage index

Cloth

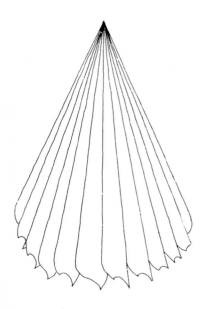

Paper

Plastic Containers

plastic bottle, (flat-sided detergent type, 24-30 oz.)
  5, 10, 11, 15, 23, 28, 35
plastic bottle, (side handle) 7, 73, 74, 76
plastic bottle, (round, no handle) 8, 22, 33, 35, 38, 46, 104
plastic buckets, (4-6 oz. size) 84
plastic buckets, (1 pt. size) 52
plastic buckets, (1 qt. size) 17, 82
plastic buckets, (1 gal. size) 17
plastic container, (large, top handle) 55
plastic creamers, 29, 39
plastic jars, (clear, screwtop) 54
plastic jug, (48 oz. size) 48, 50, 72
plastic jug, (64 oz. size) 8, 22, 44, 45, 47
plastic jug, (gal. size) 17, 35, 38, 74, 77

Miscellaneous Plastics

bags, 80, 111
berry boxes, 28, 29, 52
cheese box, (small, round) 29
coffee cups, 64
cutlery & swizzle sticks, 39, 104
deodorant holder, 29
drinking straws, 18, 94
egg-shaped nylon package, 29, 93
mesh holder for dishwasher water-softener, 29

Styrofoam

cups, 64
egg cartons, 28, 29, 52, 62, 63, 94, 100, 101
meat trays, 30, 34, 91, 92, 101, 102
packing chunks, 11, 22, 72, 92

Miscellaneous Garbage

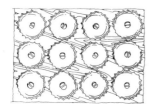

bottle caps, 19, 49
candle stubs, 82
chicken-wire fencing, 102
coat hangers, (wire) 10, 49, 76, 80, 87, 90, 92, 102, 104